We dedicate this book to Jordan, Richard, Emma, Jamie, Miles, Jason, Lisa, Charlie, Theo and Ellis

CONTENTS

ABOUT THE AUTHORS

Christine Hobart and Jill Frankel come from a background of health visiting and nursery education. They worked together in Camden before meeting again at City and Islington College. They have worked together for many years, training students to work with young children and have written twelve books encompassing all areas of the childcare curriculum. Christine is an external examiner for CACHE.

Miranda Walker has worked with children from birth to 16 years in a range of settings, including her own day nursery and out of school clubs. She has inspected nursery provision for Ofsted, and worked at East Devon College as an Early Years and Playwork lecturer and NVQ assessor and internal verifier. She is a regular contributor to industry magazines and an established author.

ACKNOWLEDGEMENTS

We would like to thank our colleagues at City and Islington College for their support and encouragement. We are particularly indebted to Angela Dare, whose clear thinking, knowledge and common sense was, as ever, generously provided. This book could not have been written without the children and families with whom we have worked and the students we have taught and from whom we have learnt so much.

Here are some acknowledgements for specific items in the book:

- The Assessment Framework on page 9 and the Principles behind the Assessment Framework on page 77 from *Framework for the Assessment of Children in Need and Their Families* (Department of Health, 2000). Crown copyright material is reproduced with the permission of the Controller of HMSO and the Queen's Printer for Scotland.
- We thank the Children's Legal Centre for the report of the inquiry into child abuse in Cleveland on page 14–15.
- 'The extent of violence involving children' on page 27 is from *Children and Violence: The Report of the Commission on Children and Violence* convened by the Gulbenkian Foundation. It is reproduced by kind permission of the Calouste Gulbenkian Foundation.
- The table on page 41 is reproduced from *Child Abuse and Neglect: An Introduction*, Workbook 1, *Making Sense of Child Abuse* by kind permission of the Open University.
- The principles from *A Policy for Young Children* (page 66) and the outline procedures on page 35 are reproduced by kind permission of the National Children's Bureau.
- The FGM report on pages 163–4 are reproduced by kind permission of Amnesty International UK. © Amnesty International 2004.
- The extract on pages 175–6 is reproduced from 'Testimony of child abuse experts under new scrutiny'. It is reproduced, with permission, from the *Sunday Herald*, 9 May 2004.
- The child protection policy in Appendix 5 is reproduced by kind permission of Bovington School, Herts.

The authors and publishers have made every effort to trace the owners of copyright material. Should copyright have been unwittingly infringed in this book, the owners should contact the publishers, who will make corrections at reprint.

THE NEEDS OF CHILDREN

The needs of children are defined by Alice Miller in her 1988 book *The Drama of Being a Child*, published by Virago Press:

1. All children are born to grow, to develop, to live, to love, and to articulate their needs and feelings for their self-protection.
2. For their development children need the respect and protection of adults who take them seriously, love them, and honestly help them to become orientated in the world.
3. When these vital needs are frustrated and children are instead abused for the sake of adults' needs by being exploited, beaten, punished, taken advantage of, manipulated, neglected, or deceived without the intervention of any witness, then their integrity will be lastingly impaired.

INTRODUCTION

Since the authors first worked together in a London borough in 1976, society has developed a greater understanding of the complex problems of child abuse and neglect. We have a much clearer view of what we can do to safeguard children and to work with children and families in partnership.

We have become aware that children of any age, sex, race, religion and socio-economic background can become victims of abuse and neglect. We now know that large numbers of children at risk are never reported to agencies that can help them and their families, and indeed, that many children thought to be at risk have not been helped. It is clear that no one professional or agency can work alone; everyone in the community must work together to effectively identify and prevent child abuse and neglect, and provide help, support and therapy for those children who have become victims and for the families involved.

This book is especially written for childcare practitioners, who are in the forefront when the abuse of young children is disclosed and are often expected to support and help the families and the children, with very little guidance. We are aware of the stress and distress caused by caring for children who have been abused or neglected and supporting their families. A sound knowledge of procedures, guidelines and good practice alongside regular access to training and supervision should aid professional practice.

1 THE HISTORY OF CHILD ABUSE

This chapter covers:
- **Historical perspectives**
- **The sixties onwards**
- **Child abuse inquiries**
- **Child sexual abuse**

It is by looking at the history of childhood that we make our judgements about child abuse today. History is used as a means of casting light on present issues. Some people feel that whatever is happening today is an improvement on the past, while others look at past centuries through rose-coloured spectacles.

We have no concrete evidence of how children were treated in earlier times. We take our ideas from contemporary paintings and literature. There were few childcare manuals, and no films or photographs to back up theories of child-rearing practices.

Historical perspectives

All historical writing is inevitably selective, and different historians have very different ideas about the concept of childhood up to the nineteenth century.

In the early part of the nineteenth century, child mortality rates were so high that it has been suggested that parents were obliged to limit the amount of emotional involvement with their young children, although this is impossible to prove. Large families were the norm, as infant mortality claimed between 50% and 75% of children before the age of 5. It was not until the mid nineteenth century that infant mortality rates decreased, thanks to better awareness of public health and sanitation.

From 1900 to 1902 there were 620–725 deaths of children aged 1 to 4. In 1995 there were 735 deaths of children in that age group.

UK infant mortality rates: deaths of infants under age 1, per thousand live births			
Period	Deaths per 1000	Period	Deaths per 1000
1900–1902	142	1990–92	7
1910–12	110	1990	7.9
1920–22	82	1991	7.4
1930–32	67	1992	6.6
1950–52	30	1993	6.3
1960–62	22	1995	6.2
1970–72	18	2004	5.22
1980–82	12		

A visit to a cemetery provides an insight into infant mortality

What seems sure is that, until the last century, children were not seen as independent citizens but as the property of their parents. This still holds true in some countries where children may be maimed by their parents to earn money by begging, or made to work from a very young age. China's policy of restricting family size to one child in urban areas has possibly led to the abandonment of girl children.

To think about
Now that it is possible to know the sex of a child before birth, should abortion of an unwanted foetus be allowed so that a child brought to term would be of the preferred gender? Do you think that this would reduce the incidence of child abuse?

Many accounts have been written over the centuries describing cruelty experienced during childhood. There are more accounts by well-educated people as they were more likely to write their experiences down, but it does not mean that abuse did not take place throughout society.

Literature often provides evidence of child abuse and infanticide. In many of his books, Charles Dickens illustrates the plight of abused and neglected children in the nineteenth century. You have only to read *Oliver Twist* or *David Copperfield* to understand what many young children endured. Charles Kingsley's *The Water Babies* describes the life of small children forced to sweep chimneys. More recently, the books of Jeannette Winterson, Maya Angelou and others describe the horrors of an unprotected childhood. Celebrities such as Oprah Winfrey and Roseanne Barr have been open about the abuse they suffered as children and this may have encouraged other survivors to speak out and to come to terms with their feelings.

Activity
Suggest two books written in the past 20 years that you have read and which describe an unhappy childhood caused by abuse or neglect.

From what we read, it seems that the distinction between children and adults was not so clear-cut as it is today. In the Middle Ages the concept of childhood did not seem to exist and once children had become physically competent between the ages of 5 and 8, they became part of the adult community and were expected to earn their keep. By the beginning of the twentieth century, concern was being expressed and the needs of children were being shown in books discussing child rearing. Legislation made children's needs and rights distinct from those of adults and by 1952 it became possible to bring care proceedings without first prosecuting the parents. Appendix 1 on page 180 is a chronology of Acts protecting children.

From 1618 to 1970 a total of 130 000 children were deported from the UK from various charitable organisations. Some of these children were temporarily in care and were sent to the colonies, in particular Australia, mostly without their family's knowledge. The average age of the children was 9.4 years and the youngest children were aged 2 years. The children were kept in ignorance of their background and were put to work as labourers or domestic servants without pay and in very primitive and often abusive circumstances.

In 1946 Caffey, a radiologist, published a paper describing patterns of multiple fractures and subdural haematoma in small children. He speculated that they could be the result of injury rather than disease. In 1953 Silverman suggested that injuries might result from parental neglect but referred to the notion of 'accident proneness'. In 1955 Woolley and Evans suggested the possibility of injury caused deliberately by parents or caregivers.

The 1960s onwards

The breakthrough in public awareness of non-accidental injury came towards the end of the 1960s and was the result of work presented by Dr Henry Kempe and his colleagues in Denver, Colorado. He was a paediatrician and his paper published in 1962 was 'The Battered Child Syndrome'. This emotive title ensured public attention. In the UK, two orthopaedic surgeons, Griffiths and Moynihan, coined the term 'battered baby'. In 1966 the British Paediatric Association published guidance to members about the management of these cases.

Public awareness of non-accidental injuries increased in the late 1960s

In 1965 Professor Keith Simpson of the Department of Forensic Medicine at the University of London published a paper referring to a father recently convicted of the murder of two of his children. Arguing that both infants were typical of battered baby syndrome, he suggested that general practitioners (GPs) should take on the role of investigator in such cases. Dr Camps at the London Hospital, another forensic scientist, argued that the incidence of this syndrome was widespread and called for the full cooperation of the medical, legal and social authorities. Until then it had mainly been the medical profession in the UK that was highlighting the issues; many of its recommendations concerned GPs and casualty doctors, insisting that they became more aware of the children at risk. Awareness outside the medical profession was very limited and members of the legal and social welfare agencies were not involved centrally. The emphasis of social work was still to keep families together and to prevent delinquency.

In 1968 the National Society for the Prevention of Cruelty to Children (NSPCC) established its Battered Child Research Unit (BCRU). BCRU published many papers between 1969 and 1977; it took on the role of educating other professional groups and ensured that the issue was taken up by the media and the government. Eventually this led to the establishment of special units. Professor John Davis, a paediatrician and chair of the Manchester Child Abuse Policy Committee, invited the submission of proposals 'to provide a specialist service'. This was to help the community services, both statutory and voluntary, deal adequately with families who severely maltreat their children, as is seen in the clinical conditions known as 'battered child syndrome'. The NSPCC unit would be available for consultation and case work where a child under the age of 4 was suspected of receiving injuries other than by accident. The first unit opened in 1972. The age range was later extended from 4 to 16.

During the 1960s and the 1970s, the emphasis was less on cruelty and punishment and more on preventative and therapeutic action. The trend was to keep families together at almost all costs and it was assumed that parents who abused must have had terrible childhoods themselves. To some extent there was a polarisation in the approach of social services and the approach of the police.

To think about
How might differences in approach militate against the police and social services working together?

In 1970 the NSPCC issued a report suggesting that the increase in publicity and professional education had led to a growth in awareness about the need for intervention in the less obvious cases of abuse. It also stressed the importance of a multidisciplinary approach and recommended the establishment of central registers of children suspected of being at risk from abuse at local level. The main function would be the identification of repeated abuse within a family and to provide therapy.

There were many terrible cases of children who died of abuse and neglect, but the case of Maria Colwell was crucial in establishing the issue as a major social problem and led to fundamental changes in policy and practice. Maria Colwell was born on 25 March 1965 and died on 7 January 1973; she was battered to death by her stepfather after she returned from foster care.

The publicity given to her brutal killing led to a change in the role of social workers. They would now take on this child protection work as the highest priority. It generated considerable concern and fear, and the media voiced disquiet about the growth, role and activities of social workers. The inquiry into Maria's death highlighted four main areas of concern:

- errors of judgement resulting from inexperience and lack of specialist knowledge for those professionally concerned with Maria's welfare;
- communication failures between the agencies, and the need to define roles and ensure they do not overlap;
- social workers have a responsibility to seek out information, but others have a responsibility not to withhold information about children at risk;
- inaccuracies and deficiencies in the recording of visits and telephone messages. Dates and times of visits must be recorded, a distinction should be made between fact and impression, and the source of all information should be made clear.

CHANGES IN PROCEDURES

At the beginning of the 1970s, various government circulars were issued advising the establishment of area review committees (ARCs), including senior representatives of all statutory and voluntary agencies. Among the terms of reference: it was suggested that:

- The duties and responsibilities of all people involved with any aspect of non-accidental injury cases should be defined.
- Local practice and procedures should be devised.
- Education and training should be provided for all professional people involved.
- Public awareness should be increased.
- Procedures should be established to ensure that children do not slip through the net if the family moves to another area.

In 1976 the government advised that all areas should hold a central register of children at risk of abuse and advised on the information that should be recorded. It stressed the importance of case conferences, now called child protection conferences, and the need to appoint a key worker to the case. Later in 1976 another circular advised that the police should attend all initial conferences. This multidisciplinary approach was consolidated in 1980 and extended the criteria for inclusion on the register from physical abuse to severe and persistent neglect and emotional abuse. Sexual abuse was not included unless associated with physical injury.

To think about
Why do you think it took so long for sexual abuse to become an issue for child protection agencies?

Circulars continued to be issued in the 1980s, emphasising the importance of a multidisciplinary response and stressing the central role of the social worker with statutory powers in the management and coordination of each case. Child abuse registers were renamed child protection registers. It was recommended that child abuse consultants or advisers should be appointed in every local authority. It was also recommended that sexual abuse should be included in the child abuse framework for the first time.

To think about
It has been said that in spite of current concern about abused children, there has never been a better time to be a child. Do you agree?

HELPLINES

The NSPCC has offered confidential help on the telephone for many years. This has been used mainly by adults reporting concerns. ChildLine was established in 1986, initiated by Esther Rantzen. She felt sure there were many children suffering from abuse of various types and unable to speak face-to-face to adult carers and she thought they would value speaking to an invisible counsellor on the telephone. She has been vindicated as there have been approximately 20 000 calls for help every year from physically and sexually abused children. Another 1 300 spoke of fear, neglect or threats made to them. While the majority of calls are

ChildLine enables a child to speak to a counsellor by telephone

about family problems, bullying, pregnancy, drug abuse or running away, one child in four is in danger from assault in some form according to ChildLine.

The role of ChildLine is to empower children to seek help for themselves, and the counsellors do not generally give direct advice. If they feel a child is in danger, they might contact the police in the child's area, but only with the permission of the child.

During the 1980s there were a number of highly publicised deaths, and social workers were often held to blame when events went tragically wrong in failing to protect children. During a short period in 1987 a large number of children in Cleveland were removed from their parents following allegations of sexual abuse. The allegations were substantiated by a rather controversial medical test. Between March 1987 and July 1987 a total of 104 children were removed from their homes. Many of these children were later thought to have been removed unnecessarily, and doctors and social workers were blamed for being overzealous. In 1997 a three-part television documentary, *The Death of Childhood*, appeared to suggest that many of the children who were returned home had in fact been abused.

CHILDREN ACT 1989

By the end of the 1980s there was concern over the conflicting areas of family privacy, the accountability of professional power and the rights of children. The Children Act 1989 was drawn up to address these areas and to make the law simpler and easier to use. The Act contains three major principles:

- The welfare of the child is paramount.
- There should be as little delay as possible by the court in deciding issues.
- The court has to be satisfied that it is better to make an order than not to do so.

The Act also introduces a 'welfare checklist' that the court has a duty to consider in any proceedings, and allows the court to have greater flexibility in its decision-making powers. This would take into account:

- the wishes and feelings of the child subject to the child's age and understanding;
- the child's physical, emotional and educational needs;
- the likely effect on the child of any change in circumstances;
- the age, gender, background and relevant characteristics of the child;
- the parents' ability to meet the child's needs;
- any harm the child has suffered or is at risk of suffering;
- the court's powers under the Children Act.

Until the mid 1960s, the family appeared to be a secure unit, and the idealised nuclear family was seen as the pivot of values and social mores. The shock of the battered baby syndrome, the death of Maria Colwell and the Cleveland affair have resulted in radical rethinking about how we perceive and support children and families who are at risk.

In 1995 the Department of Health published *Child Protection: Messages from Research*. This reviewed 20 different research projects on child protection issues and asked the following questions:

- Was the multi-agency approach operating effectively for children on the child protection register?
- Was there an appropriate response to emotional abuse and neglect?
- Were agencies concentrating on incidents rather than the children's wider developmental needs?
- How do we define the threshold in relation to who enters the child protection system?

It also raised some wider points:

- Professionals were often unclear about their role.
- The training of professionals was often inadequate for the responsibilities involved.
- The children and their families often felt they had little involvement or influence in critical decisions that were being made, so the outcomes were less successful.

In 1997 *Childhood Matters*, the findings of the National Commission of Inquiry into the Prevention of Child Abuse tried to move the debate on to issues of prevention and to wider concepts of harm.

In 1999 the government published *Working Together to Safeguard Children*, presenting a national framework for child protection practice for everyone working with children and families. It set out the responsibilities of the agencies and the procedures to follow when there were concerns about a child. It was accompanied by *Framework for the Assessment of Children in Need and their Families*, suggesting that child protection practice should operate within a broader framework of children in need. This document encouraged:

- the need to recognise a family's strengths as well weaknesses;
- an integrated approach to protecting children, responding to their wider developmental needs;

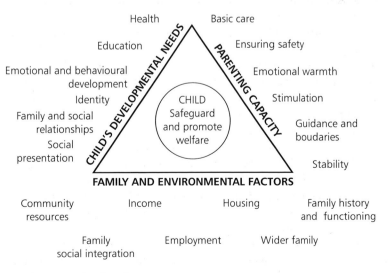

Assessment framework triangle

- a consistent approach to all children in need;
- a common language shared by all professionals to be used at all stages of referral, assessment and planning.

The Protection of Children Act 1999 enabled the Criminal Records Bureau to disclose information about people who are included on the Protection of Children Act List, or List 99, along with their criminal records. The Act provides for a 'one-stop shop' system of checking people seeking to work with children. It requires childcare organisations proposing to employ someone in a childcare setting to ensure individuals are checked and not to employ anyone who is included on the list. List 99 is held by the Teacher Misconduct Team at the Department for Education and Skills (DfES). A similar list is held by the Department of Health (DH). The Criminal Records Bureau provides three level of checking:

- *Basic disclosure* is a criminal conviction certificate that excludes conviction spent under the Rehabilitation of Offenders Act 1974, or cautions; only the job applicant can apply for such a check and can choose whether to show it to the employer.
- *Standard disclosure* shows details of all convictions on record, cautions, reprimands and warnings. It will also give information from the DfES and DH lists.
- *Enhanced disclosure* shows the same details as standard disclosure plus a check with local police forces for any additional relevant information.

In 2000 the Children and Young Persons Unit was established to administer the Children's Fund finance for projects to improve services for children.

In September 2001 the regulation of all early years provision was taken over by the Early Years Directorate within the Office for Standards in Education (Ofsted). All eligible childcare providers were required to be registered by Ofsted and had to meet the DfES National Standards which represented quality of care and education at that time. Standard 13 referred to child protection and stated: 'The registered person complies with local child protection procedures approved by the Area Child Protection Committee and ensures that all adults working and looking after children in the provision are able to put the procedures into practice.'

In January 2003 the Laming Report, looking at the death of Victoria Climbié, found that health, police and social services missed 12 opportunities to save her. In September 2003 the government published *Every Child Matters*, a Green Paper proposing:

- 150 children's trusts to be set up by 2006;
- the amalgamation of health, education and social services;
- a children's director to oversee local services;
- statutory local children's boards to replace existing area child protection committees;
- a children's commissioner for England;
- an electronic tracking system for England's children.

It went on to say, 'Child Protection cannot be separated from policies to improve children's lives as a whole. We need to focus both on the universal services which every child uses and on more targeted services for those with additional needs.'

The Children Act 2004 implemented the recommendations of *Every Child Matters*:

- Children's commissioners were appointed in England, Wales, Scotland and Northern Ireland. Their job is to raise awareness of the best interests of children and young people and report annually to Parliament.
- Local authorities have a duty to make arrangements to promote cooperation between agencies (social services, health, education and the justice system) in order to improve children's well-being. Key partners have a duty to take part in these arrangements.
- Key agencies that work with children have a duty to put in place arrangements to make sure that they take account of the need to safeguard and promote the welfare of children when doing their jobs.
- Databases contain basic information on children and young people to help professionals in working together to provide early support to children, young people and their families. Case details are not included.
- Local authorities have set up Statutory Local Safeguarding Children Boards and ensure that key partners take part.
- Local authorities are required to appoint a director of children's services and a lead member to be responsible for, as a minimum, education and children's social services functions.
- There is an integrated inspection framework and provision for regular joint area reviews to be carried out to look at how children's services as a whole operate across each local authority area.

Implementation of the Act was phased in between 2005 and 2007. Also see page 48 for further information about *Every Child Matters*.

The Childcare Act 2006 was passed to introduce a curriculum framework called the *Early Years Foundation Stage* (EYFS) and to support settings in providing high quality, integrated care and education for children aged 0–5 years. It also gave local authorities the responsibility to improve outcomes for all children under five. The overarching aim of the EYFS is to help young children achieve the five *Every Child Matters* outcomes by:

- **setting standards** for the learning, development and care young children should experience when they attend a setting outside their family home. Every child should make progress, with no children left behind.
- **providing equality of opportunity and anti-discriminatory practice**. Ensuring that every child is included and not disadvantaged because of ethnicity, culture, religion, home language, family background, learning difficulties or disabilities, gender or ability.
- **creating a framework for partnership working between parents and professionals**, and between all the settings that the child attends.
- **improving quality and consistency in the early years** through standards that apply to all settings. This provides the basis for the inspection and regulation regime carried out by Ofsted.
- **laying a secure foundation for future learning** through learning and develop-

ment that is planned around the individual needs and interests of the child. This is informed by the use of on-going observational assessment.

Since 2008, The Early Years Foundation Stage has been mandatory for:

- all schools
- all early years providers in Ofsted registered settings.

It applies to children from birth to the end of the academic year in which the child has their fifth birthday. Visit www.everychildmatters.gov.uk and www.standards.dfes.gov.uk/eyfs for further details.

Procedures for registration and inspection of childcare providers changed in 2007/2008, when the National Standards were made defunct. There are now two registers, the **Childcare Register** which has a compulsory part and a voluntary part, and the **Early Years Register**. Registered settings must comply with the Requirements of the Childcare Register, and if they deliver the EYFS, the EYFS Welfare Requirements. For further details see page 181.

Child abuse inquiries

There are three main types of inquiry:

- an internal inquiry or case review, conducted by senior managers of all concerned agencies;
- an external inquiry set up locally, but with an independent chairperson and often with members from outside the area;
- a statutory inquiry set up by government.

An inquiry will try to:

- establish the true facts of the case;
- determine who was responsible for carrying out certain actions and neglecting others;
- look critically at the quality of the work and collaboration of the relevant agencies;
- learn from the experience and recommend changes in legislation, professional responsibilities and governmental guidelines;
- restore confidence in the system and reassure the general public.

INQUIRIES

In your reading and training as a childcare practitioner, you may come across children whose death from physical abuse or neglect resulted in an inquiry.

Maria Colwell, aged 8, was killed by her stepfather in 1973, shortly after being returned home from her foster parents. Neighbours and her school reported evidence of rejection and physical abuse. She was subject to a supervision order at the time of her death.

In 1974 Susan Auckland, aged 15 months, was killed by her father. At the end of the trial it was stated that he had also killed his 9-week-old daughter, Marianne, in 1968. The father was sentenced to five years' imprisonment for manslaughter.

Jasmine Beckford, aged 4, was killed by her stepfather in July 1984. She was neglected and abused over a long period by both parents. Jasmine had attended a nursery but had very poor attendance. She was withdrawn from the nursery 10 months before her death. She was in the care of the local authority when she was killed.

Tyra Henry, aged 22 months, was killed by her father in September 1984, while still legally in the care of the local authority. Her mother became pregnant with Tyra's brother Tyrone, at the age of 15. The father assaulted Tyrone when he was 4 months old, leaving him blind and brain damaged, and he was removed into long-term care. The father was convicted of cruelty and later a care order was made on Tyra when she was born. She remained on this care order at the time of her death.

Kimberley Carlile, aged 4½ years, was killed by her stepfather in 1986. She had been tortured and starved for many weeks before her death. There were concerns while the family was living in the Wirral. When they moved to Greenwich, social services attempted to monitor the family but found it difficult to gain access.

Heidi Koseda died due to the neglect of her mother and her mother's partner in 1985. She had been well cared for until her parents separated when she was 2, and her mother began to live with a man known for his violent behaviour. Neighbours had complained to the NSPCC that Heidi had not been seen. She was locked away in a room and died of starvation. It was two months before her body was found.

Rikki Neave, aged 6, was found dead in 1994. His mother was cleared of his murder but given seven years' imprisonment for cruelty. The report carried out in 1997 by social services inspectors stated that the fault lay primarily with senior management in Cambridgeshire Social Services.

Chelsea Brown, aged 2, was battered to death by her father in 1999. He had a criminal record for violence against children. The social worker had visited the family 27 times in the 10 weeks before her death and had taken Chelsea to a paediatrician who said that six out of nine areas of bruising had no plausible explanation and at least one was deliberately inflicted. These events should have triggered police involvement and a multi-agency case conference under local procedures, but neither happened.

Lauren Wright, aged 6, was found dead in 2000 following a fatal punch or kick from her stepmother. Norfolk social services admitted that it made several mistakes and missed opportunities to save Lauren.

Victoria Climbié, aged 8 years, died in 2000 from hyperthermia after suffering months of abuse and neglect. The public inquiry heard that there were at least 12 chances for the agencies involved in her protection to have saved her. The outcry about her death led to the Laming Report and yet more reform of child protection services.

Ainlee Labonte, aged 2, was starved and tortured to death by her parents in 2002. She had 64 scars and bruises on her body when she died weighing just 21 pounds. In addition to poor communication, weak risk assessment and inadequate coordination of the agencies involved, the excessive violence of the parents intimidated the agencies and the neighbours.

In August 2007, 17-month-old 'Baby P' died in North London while on the child protection register. He had suffered over fifty injuries in his short life, and in an eight month period he had received sixty visits from social workers, police and doctors.

The local authority involved was Haringey Council, the same council which was criticised in the Laming Report following the Victoria Climbié case. (The head of Children's Services in Haringey was subsequently sacked). Lord Laming was commissioned by the Children's Secretary to carry out a review into how well local authorities have adopted the reforms introduced as a result of his original report.

In March 2009, Laming reported that while there was "overwhelming support" for Every Child Matters, "significant problems" remain in working between different child protection agencies. He reported that social services departments suffer from "low staff morale, poor supervision, high caseloads, under-resourcing and inadequate training" and made 58 recommendations on how to bring about change in protecting children from harm. These include a reduction in the time it takes for care of children cases to come to court, actions to rectify the "inadequate" training of social workers, a call for Government to take charge of driving reforms for child protection and the establishment of a new 'National Safeguarding Delivery Unit' – a Whitehall body to pressure ministers for effective reform. For further information and updates about the Unit, visit www.nspcc.org.uk/Inform/nsu_wda63026.html.

In 2008, Children's Services and police in East London were criticised after six-month-old 'Baby H' was killed by her father in the Borough of Redbridge. The family had previously lived in Tower Hamlets. Despite the mother reporting the father to police when he pinched Baby H at the age of two months, no protective action was taken. A Serious Case Review followed, in which a social worker in Tower Hamlets was criticised for delays in commencing the Initial Review of the family, and for failing to mention concerns about Baby H to colleagues in Redbridge when the family moved. Baby H died when her father smashed her head on the floor after she refused to eat a yoghurt. This happened in the year in which Tower Hamlets council was awarded 'beacon status' by the Government for 'early intervention, children at risk' policies.

Activity

You will probably have in your family people who will remember the death of Maria Colwell. Did they feel shocked at the time? Who did they blame and do they think it could happen today?

Activity

Research into one of the above cases. Use your research to answer the following questions:

- What agencies were involved in the case? Comment on how well they worked together.
- What signs of concern were evident before the child's death?
- Had the child's health and development been monitored?
- Were there any important cultural factors?
- Were there any signs of stereotyping?
- Did the case change future practice and legislation?

Child sexual abuse

Until the 1980s, the realisation that young children from birth onwards could be sexually abused had not been recognised by the general public or by many professionals. In 1986 ChildLine was established and, for the first time, the public was made aware that very young children were disclosing sexual abuse.

To think about

In any community where there is a case of sexual abuse, what impact would this have on a local nursery? What would be the role of the child-care practitioner?

In 1987 Hobbs and Wynne, two doctors working in Cleveland, published an influential paper presenting evidence that boys as well as girls were sexually abused and that very small children, even babies, might be victims of such abuse. It was also apparent that it occurred in all sections of society. In the same year, a newspaper reported that a large number of angry parents had their children removed from their care on the basis of a medical diagnosis carried out by two consultant paediatricians. Procedures did not exist to cope with the:

■ conflicting medical opinions;
■ spiralling referrals from different agencies;
■ conflict over the correct method of examination;
■ extent and nature of parental involvement;
■ failure of communication;
■ overfull hospital wards;
■ distraught parents and upset children.

An inquiry was set up into the events at Cleveland and its recommendations were summarised by a briefing from the Children's Legal Centre (see below).

The fact that a child does not die from sexual abuse means that, although the perpetrator may be brought to court, there is rarely a local or an official inquiry. It is only when a number of children are involved, as in the Cleveland inquiry (121 children), or in organised abuse (sometimes referred to as satanic or ritual abuse) as in Nottingham in 1988 (23 children), Rochdale in 1991 (20 children), Manchester in 1991 (13 children) and the Orkney Islands in 1991 (9 children) that the media becomes involved and public awareness is aroused. There have been a number of inquiries into abuse in residential homes, again involving large numbers of children.

THE CLEVELAND INQUIRY REPORT'S RECOMMENDATIONS ON CHILDREN

There is a danger that in looking to the welfare of the children believed to be the victims of sexual abuse the children themselves may be overlooked. The child is a person and not "an object of concern". We recommend that:

a Professionals recognise the need for adults to explain to children what is going on. Children are entitled to a proper explanation appropriate to their age, to be told why they are being taken away from home and given some idea of what is going to happen to them.

b Professionals should not make promises which cannot be kept to a child, and in the light of possible court proceedings should not promise a child that what is said in confidence can be kept in confidence.

c Professionals should always listen carefully to what the child has to say and take seriously what is said.

d Throughout the proceedings the views and the wishes of the child particularly as to what should happen to him/her, should be taken into consideration by the professionals involved with their problems.

e The views and wishes of the child should be placed before whichever court deals with the case. We do not, however, suggest that those wishes should predominate.

f Children should not be subjected to repeated medical examinations solely for evidential purposes. Where appropriate, according to age and understanding, the consent of the child should be obtained before any medical examination or photography.

g Children should not be subjected to repeated interviews nor to the probing and confrontational type of 'disclosure' interview for the same purpose, for it in itself can be damaging and harmful to them. The consent of the child should where possible be obtained before the interviews are recorded on video.

h The child should be medically examined and interviewed in a suitable and sensitive environment, where there are suitably trained staff available.

i When a child is moved from home or between hospital and foster home it is important that those responsible for the day-to-day care of the child not only understand the child's legal status but also have sufficient information to look after the child properly.

j Those involved in investigation of child sexual abuse should make a conscious effort to ensure that they act throughout in the best interests of the child.

We have seen in this chapter how infant mortality has been dramatically reduced in the past century and how society has responded to distressing cases of child abuse. Many child protection issues remain to be addressed. *Child Protection: Messages from Research* identified three main areas of interest:

- How is abuse defined in the context of normal childhood experience, and how do we estimate the incidence of different types of abuse and neglect in society?
- How can we achieve the protection and safety of children, and who is involved in this process?
- How can we establish good practice in all stages of the child protection process?

As a professional childcare practitioner, you will be alert to all issues concerning children and keep up to date in your reading. Practice and procedures used to protect children are constantly being evaluated and reassessed in the light of current research and debate. Children have many needs: love, shelter, stimulation, security and nourishment, but meeting these needs counts for nothing unless children are adequately protected.

KEY TERMS

You need to know what these words and phrases mean:

battered baby
central register
infant mortality rate
multidisciplinary approach
non-accidental injury
nuclear family
preventative and therapeutic action
professional childcare practitioner

Resources

Aries, P. (1996) *Centuries of Childhood*. Pimlico, London.
Ferguson, H. (2004) *Protecting Children in Time*. Palgrave, Basingstoke, Hants.
Fletcher, A. and Hussey, S. (1999) *Childhood in Question*. Manchester University Press, Manchester.
Foley, P., Roche, J. and Tucker, S. (eds) (2001) *Children in Society*. Oxford University Press, Oxford.
Heywood, C. (2003) *A History of Childhood*. Polity, Cambridge.
Holland, P. (2004) *Picturing Childhood*. I. B. Tauris, London.
Jenks, C. (2005) *Childhood*. 2nd Edition, Routledge, London.
Kempe, R. S. and Kempe, C. H. *(1978) Child Abuse*. Fontana, London.
Prout, A. (2005) *The Future of Childhood*. Routledge, London.
Reder, P., Duncan, S. and Gray, M. (1993) *Beyond Blame*. Routledge, London.
Reid, D. H. S. (1992) *Suffer the Little Children (Orkney Child Abuse Scandal)*. Medical Institute for Research in Child Cruelty.
Sinclair, R. and Bullock, R. (2002) *Learning from Past Experience*. Department of Health, London.

WEBSITE

www.everychildmatters.gov.uk

2 *DEFINING ABUSE*

During your career as a childcare practitioner you will probably come into contact with more than one child who is being neglected or abused. You will find this distressing and, as a professional person, you will need to have some idea why this happens, how to recognise abuse, what procedures to follow, and how to help the child and the family. Child abuse may be difficult to define but a clear understanding is necessary so that you may act with confidence when working with vulnerable children.

The needs of children

During your training you will have become familiar with the needs of children, so as to ensure optimum growth and development. If these needs are not met, children will not thrive. These needs are shown in Maslow's hierachy of needs (page 20 and by the assessment framework triangle (page 9).

Working Together to Safeguard Children was published by the Department of Health in 1999. It states that all children deserve the opportunity to achieve their potential. They should be enabled to:
- be as physically and mentally healthy as possible;
- gain the maximum benefit possible from good quality educational opportunities;
- live in a safe environment and be protected from harm;
- experience emotional well-being;
- feel loved and valued and be supported by a network of reliable and affectionate relationships;
- become competent in looking after themselves and coping with everyday living;
- have a positive image of themselves and a secure sense of identity;
- develop good interpersonal skills and confidence in social situations.

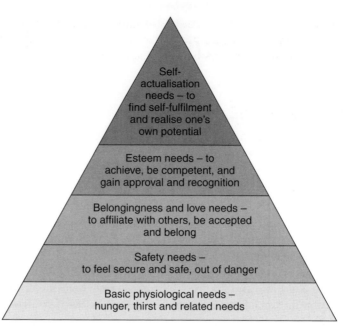

Maslow's hierarchy of needs

Defining child abuse

Abuse or neglect may occur deliberately or by failure to safeguard children. There are some commonly accepted definitions of child abuse, but when looking at a number of local authority child protection documents you will see a variety of definitions. The broad categories are neglect, physical abuse and injury, emotional abuse and sexual abuse, but all these categories overlap and interconnect.

Kidscape, a national registered charity, is an organisation which enables children to learn strategies to keep themselves safe and offers one way of defining abuse. According to Kidscape, 'Child abuse is making a child feel unwanted, ugly, worthless, guilty, unloved; being physically violent to a child; exploiting a child sexually; failing to provide the things needed for a child to grow.'

Activity
Obtain a copy of your local authority's child protection procedures. How are the areas of abuse defined?

To think about
Should everybody be obliged by law to report suspected child abuse? Do you think a national campaign showing violent, distressing images of abused children raises public awareness and encourages people to report suspected abuse?

The report *Childhood Matters*, defines abuse like this: 'Child abuse consists of anything which individuals, institutions or processes do or fail to do, which directly or indirectly harms children or damages their prospects of safe and healthy development.'

PHYSICAL ABUSE AND INJURY

Physical abuse of children is the intentional, non-accidental use of physical force and violence, resulting in hurting, injuring, hitting, shaking, throwing, poisoning, burning or scalding, drowning, suffocating or destroying the child. Most at risk are children under age 2 but children of all ages may become victims.

SHAKEN IMPACT SYNDROME

Shaken impact syndrome describes injury caused by shaking. Babies under one year are the most vulnerable as their underdeveloped neck muscles are too weak to support their large and heavy heads. The brain and surrounding blood vessels are immature and fragile. Shaking causes the brain to move within the skull, causing the blood vessels to tear and blood to flood into the skull. The long-term effects can include:

- visual impairment;
- hearing impairment;
- seizures;
- learning difficulties;
- brain damage.

Shaking is usually triggered by a child's persistent crying.

In 2000 a Scottish study suggested that up to 170 babies may be injured each year in the UK by being shaken violently by their parents or carers. Some die and nearly 80% of the survivors are left with long-term learning difficulties, seizures and problems with movement.

In 2001 the neural damage in 53 children aged between 20 days and 8 years was studied by a group in Sheffield and London. They had died after non-accidental head injuries. The researchers were looking for a symptom known as diffuse axonal injury (DAI), thought to occur if severe force is applied to the brain by violent shaking or falls from heights. The researchers found that in the majority of cases the doctors had not diagnosed DAI, but examination of the brains revealed signs of damage due to the brain stretching where it joined the spinal cord; this is the sort of injury that could occur if a baby's head is allowed to flop backwards and forwards. It could lead to serious breathing problems causing oxygen starvation and eventual death. Contrary to previous thought, it was concluded that the shaking need not be violent to cause fatal injury in a baby. This was confirmed in 2005 by Professor Helen Whitwell, a forensic pathologist, who challenged the diagnostic test saying it was no longer safe to determine that the baby had been abused by shaking.

NEGLECT

Neglect is failure by the parents or carers to provide adequately for the physical and psychological needs and safety of their children; it is not always intentional. Some parents or carers put their own needs and interests first and neglect the child, whereas others might be unwell or unable to cope, in particular with the changing needs of the developing child. All children are vulnerable, but the preschool child is most at risk. Neglect, thought to be five times more prevalent than physical abuse, is difficult to diagnose as it has to continue for quite a long time before the effects are visible. It is not only the very dirty, hungry child who is neglected — the term includes abandoning children for periods of time, emotional and educational neglect, denying medical care and treatment, and not providing a secure environment. There have been several reported incidents of parents going on holiday and leaving their children inadequately cared for. Long-term consequences of neglect can result in cycles of deprivation continuing from generation to generation.

Neglect may be five times more prevalent than physical abuse

SEXUAL ABUSE

According to Schechter and Roberge, sexual abuse is the 'involvement of dependent, developmentally immature children or adolescents in sexual activities that they do not truly comprehend, to which they are unable to give informed consent, or that violate the social taboos of family roles. In other words, it is the use of children by adults for sexual gratification'. Sexual abuse may involve physical contact, or non-contact activities such as looking at pornographic material or encouraging children to behave in sexually inappropriate ways. It can occur in any age group with boys or girls, perpetrated by men or women. Sexual abuse is an abuse of power and the responsibility rests entirely with the perpetrator. It involves either force or emotional manipulation.

A leaflet from NCH Action for Children states that in March 1994 there were 9 600 children registered under the sexual abuse category on child protection registers — just over one-quarter of all cases registered.

EMOTIONAL ABUSE

Some level of emotional abuse is involved in all types of abuse, but it may occur on its own. It is the persistent emotionally cruel treatment of a child so as to hinder the child's emotional development and mental health. The child might be isolated from their peer group and ignored by family members. Children of any age group may be exposed to constant criticism and hostility, and lack of affection and warmth. They may be rejected or extremely overprotected. They often suffer from poor self-esteem and lack confidence. They may feel frightened and in danger.

FAILURE TO THRIVE

Failure to thrive occurs when a child fails to gain weight or to grow and achieve their expected weight and height. This is always due to inadequate intake of

Regular monitoring may reveal failure to thrive

calories. Children who have no medical or physical reason not to develop normally may fail to thrive, because they have a negative relationship with the parent or carer. This is likely to be picked up in the younger age group, when children are regularly monitored and attending health clinics.

Activity
Obtain and discuss documentation used by health-care professionals to monitor children's growth and development.

ORGANISED ABUSE

Organised abuse generally refers to sexual abuse and may involve physical injury or even death. There will be a number of perpetrators and a number of abused children. There is an element of deliberate planning. It may refer to a paedophile ring, prostitution or the involvement of children in the production of pornographic material, and may include an element of ritual or the occult. This might be used to instil fear in the victims and so ensure secrecy. The extent of ritual or satanic abuse is disputed.

To think about
How appropriate is it to celebrate Halloween with very young children?

FACTITIOUS OR FABRICATED ILLNESS

Previously known as Munchausen syndrome by proxy, factitious illness has been defined as:
- intentional production or feigning of physical or psychological signs or symptoms in another person who is under the individual's care;
- the motivation for the perpetrator's behaviour is to assume the sick role by proxy;
- external incentives for the behaviour, such as economic gain, avoiding legal responsibility, or improving physical well-being are absent.

Children most at risk of this abuse are aged 15 months to 6 years. Many different medical opinions are sought, and symptoms are induced in the child to deceive the doctors. It is linked with physical abuse and may include poisoning. The parent wishes to be looked on as a good parent, caring and attentive to their child.

To think about
Would you extend any of the definitions of abuse and neglect?

SIGNIFICANT HARM

The concept of 'significant harm' is embodied in Section 31(2) of the Children Act 1989:

A court may only make a care order or supervision order if it is satisfied (a) that the child concerned is suffering or is likely to suffer, significant harm; (b) that the harm or likelihood of harm, is attributable to (i) the care given to the child, or likely to be given to him if the order were not made, not being what it would be reasonable to expect a parent to give him, (ii) the child's being beyond parental control.

The guide on page 26 considers the amount of harm by looking at the effect the abuse has had on the individual child's normal development.

Working Together to Safeguard Children states that to understand and establish significant harm it is necessary to consider:
- the family context;
- the child's development within the context of their family and wider social environment;
- any special needs, such as a medical condition, a communication difficulty or disability that may affect the child's development and care within the family;
- the nature of harm, in terms of ill-treatment or failure to provide adequate care;
- the impact on the child's health and development;
- the adequacy of parental care.

As a generalisation, the more abusive the child's experience, the greater deviation from normal growth and development can be expected. Abusing a child can include many categories: a child who is physically neglected may well be starved of love as well as food; a child who is sexually abused may also be physically injured and emotionally distressed. This overlap will become apparent when we look at how to recognise abuse (Chapter 4).

DOMESTIC VIOLENCE

Domestic violence takes place in the home and is violence directed against a current or former partner and often involves the children in the household. It is usually physical and can also be a way of controlling and dominating a relationship. It is rarely a one-off event and it can also include emotional and verbal abuse. The perpetrator is usually male.

Statistics

NSPCC

According to the NSPCC, an estimated 150–200 children die each year in England and Wales following incidents of abuse or neglect. Thousands more suffer long-term emotional and psychological problems because of ill-treatment by their parents or those looking after them.

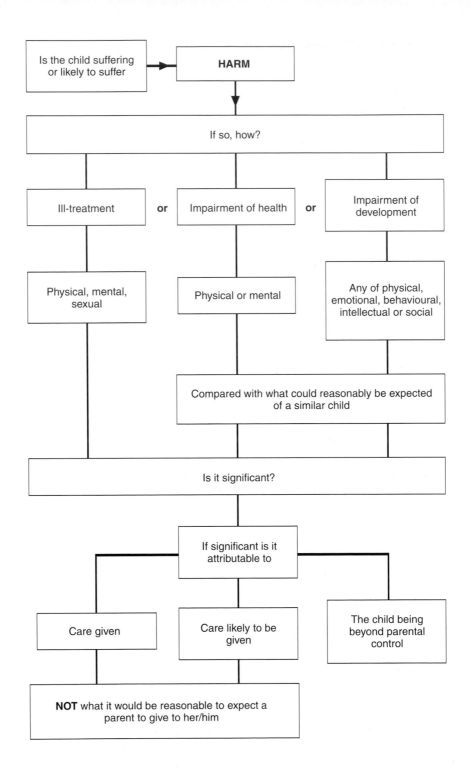

Significant harm criteria

The NSPCC research department produces information for the NSPCC website which shows that measuring the prevalence or incidence of child abuse in a country requires an understanding of what child abuse is, how it is recognised and how it is recorded:

- prevalence of child abuse refers to the proportion of the defined population (usually adult) who have been abused during a specified time period, usually childhood;
- incidence refers to the number of new cases occurring in a defined population (usually children) over a year.

Understanding

Child abuse is a culturally defined phenomenon. Kempe commented on 'the rights of a child to be protected from parents unable to cope at a level assumed to be reasonable by the society in which they reside'. What is regarded as 'reasonable' changes within and between societies. In a country where a large proportion of the child population is afflicted by malnutrition, a parent's inability to provide sufficient food to their child would not be categorised as neglect on the parent's part. In more affluent countries there have been changes in the recognition of the potentially abusive nature of some behaviours, which were previously accepted as 'reasonable'. A 1995 survey by Creighton and Russell of the childhood experiences of a national UK sample of adults aged 18–45 found that some 35% said they had been hit with an implement. Only 7% felt that it was acceptable to do that to a child now. Within any society there is continual evolution of the parental behaviours that are deemed unacceptable towards children.

Recognition and recording

The most popular analogy for child abuse is an iceberg — only a fraction of the whole is visible. We can divide the iceberg into layers:

- *Layer 1*: children whose abuse is recorded in the criminal statistics of a country.
- *Layer 2*: children who are officially recorded as being in need of protection from abuse, e.g. children on child protection registers in England or substantiated child abuse cases in the US.
- *Layer 3*: children who have been reported to child protection agencies by the general public, or other professionals such as teachers or doctors, but who have not been registered.
- *Layer 4*: abused or neglected children who are recognised as such by relatives or neighbours but are not reported to any professional agency.
- *Layer 5*: children who have not been recognised as abused or neglected by anyone, including the victims and the perpetrators.

UK government figures can be provided for Layers 1 to 3:

- *Layer 1*: from 1 April 2007 to 31 March 2008 there were 5,299 reported offences of 'cruelty to or neglect of children', 1,118 offences of sexual assault of a male under 13 and 3,976 offences of sexual assault of a female.
- *Layer 2*: in *Working Together to Safeguard Children 2006* the government announced that the maintenance of a separate child protection register would be phased out by 1st April 2008. It has been replaced by the Integrated

Children's System (ICS) and the existence of a child protection plan. In 2008 29,200 children were the subject of a child protection plan in England and 2,320 in Wales.

■ *Layer 3*: there were 552,000 referrals concerning child maltreatment to social services departments in England during the year ending 31 March 2005. (*DfES, 2004*)

CHILDLINE

ChildLine's annual report for 2007 reveals that 159,535 children were counselled and thousands more received straightforward advice; 4 000 children called every day, of whom 1800 were put through to counsellors. In 2007:

■ 12,453 calls concerned physical abuse.
■ 13,237 concerned sexual abuse; 59% of the perpetrators were within the caller's family, 29% of perpetrators were known but not in the family, and 4% were strangers.
■ 37,074 received advice on bullying.
■ 21,088 described family tensions.
■ 289 children reported domestic violence.
■ 2,636 children reported other abuse (risk, neglect, emotional).
■ 11,375 children reported concern for others.

In 1995 the Gulbenkian Foundation published a report on the incidence of violence to children (page 29).

The report *Children and Violence* followed a two-year evidence-gathering exercise involving over 10 000 individuals and organisations. They received over 1,000 letters from survivors of child abuse. Of these, 80% said they had been sexually abused. Only 32% said they had told anyone and 13% had never revealed what had happened. The evidence showed the abuse often began at preschool age and continued well into adolescence. The report stated that £1 billion was a conservative estimate for the annual cost of abuse but said it was impossible to assess accurately because abuse has such long-term effects.

EXTENT OF VIOLENCE INVOLVING CHILDREN

Children are far more often victims of violence than perpetrators of violence, and certain children are particularly at risk, including disabled children and some ethnic groups. One of the most disturbing social statistics is that the risk of homicide for babies under the age of 1 is almost four times as great as for any other age group. There is increasing knowledge about violence to children and greater sensitivity towards it, particularly sexual abuse, bullying and other violence in institutions. It is not possible to tell whether these forms of violence have increased in incidence or become more visible. There are problems about building any accurate picture of violence to children within families, but the most recent UK research shows that a substantial minority of children suffer severe physical punishment; most children are hit by their parents, up to one-third of younger children more than once a week.

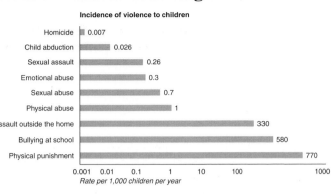
Only a very small proportion of children — mostly male but with an increasing minority of young women — get involved in committing violent offences. Very roughly, 4 per 1,000 young people aged between 10 and 18 are cautioned or convicted for offences involving violence against the person.

It appears that children's involvement in some but not all crimes of violence in the UK has increased over the past decade. But in comparison with the US, overall levels of interpersonal violence in the UK are very low, and there is recent evidence that in comparison with some European countries, levels of self-reported violence by children in the UK are also low.

Recent Home Office figures show that domestic violence claims 150 lives each year, it accounts for one-quarter of all violent crime, on average there will be 35 assaults before a victim calls the police, and it claims the lives of two women each week. It costs in excess of £5 million a year. It is estimated that 1 in 4 women may experience violence in their relationships with men

A Hackney study, *Links Between Domestic Violence and Child Abuse*, showed that half the women killed each year were killed by partners, and 100 000 women each year seek medical help for injuries caused by partners. A Home Office violent crime survey in 1989 showed that 25% of all assaults recorded by the police were domestic violence offences and around 10–15% of cases were of violence against the person.

In an NCH Action for Children study in 1994 one-quarter of the mothers said that their violent partners had also physically assaulted their children. Several said that the children had been sexually abused. More than 5 in 6 of the mothers thought that the children had been affected by the violence in the longer term. Many of the children showed signs and behaviour indicators of emotional abuse.

In November 2004 the Domestic Violence Crime and Victims Act came into being. It makes it easier for the Crown Prosecution Service (CPS) to prosecute the perpetrator and more difficult for the perpetrator to reoffend. Common assault is now an arrestable offence, allowing the police to remove the perpetrator from the scene more easily. Breaking a non-molestation order is a criminal offence with a penalty of up to five years in prison. Restraining orders may now be granted even after an acquittal if the court thinks it is necessary. The CPS is now able to take the decision to prosecute with or without the permission of the victim. A prosecution will not automatically be dropped if the victim withdraws their statement.

CASE STUDY 2.1

You are working in Year 2 of an infant school and Marlon, aged 7, is one the pupils. He is becoming uncontrollable in class, continually fighting, refusing to do as he is told by female staff and his mother. He tells the other children about violent videos that he watches at home with his father. He looks tired and has told you that he finds it difficult to sleep and that when he does he has bad dreams. You are aware that his mother is in a violent relationship. The police are often called to the house and the neighbours have been in touch with the NSPCC. In spite of advice, the mother seems unable to leave her violent partner.

1 What might you do to help Marlon?
2 What support might you give the mother?
3 With whom might you discuss the family?
4 What is likely to happen now that the NSPCC has become involved?

Activity

As you read your newspaper and professional magazines, note and record any statistical information. Looking at the separate areas of abuse, identify any upward or downward trends. If you have access to the Internet, compare the figures in the US, Australia and Canada with those of the UK.

Problems of definition

Defining child abuse is not an exact concept. Thresholds, in particular, can be subjective. A threshold is the point when a child generates sufficient concern to be deemed in need of protection, and the child protection agencies become involved. For example, when does smacking become hitting? When does demonstrative affection become a sexual assault? You will need to consider all these points if you ever suspect abuse of a child in your care.

The 1995 study *Child Protection: Messages from Research* made the following points:

- Child abuse is difficult to define, but clear parameters for intervention are necessary if professionals are to act with confidence to protect vulnerable children.
- Thresholds which legitimise action on the part of child protection agencies appear as the most important components of any definition of child abuse.
- The research evidence suggests that authoritative knowledge about what is known to be bad for children should play a greater part in drawing these thresholds.
- A large number of children in need live in contexts in which their health and development are neglected. For these children it is the corrosiveness of long-term emotional, physical and occasionally sexual maltreatment that causes psychological impairment or even significant harm.
- Instances of child sexual abuse may not conform to general findings about child protection. For example, minor single incidents can damage children, and thresholds and criminal statutes tend to be clearer than is found when dealing with physical abuse.

KEY TERMS

You need to know what these words and phrases mean:

> domestic violence
> educational abuse
> emotional abuse
> factitious illness
> failure to thrive
> Kidscape
> neglect
> organised abuse
> physical abuse and injury
> pornography
> sexual abuse
> shaken impact syndrome
> significant harm

Resources

Jones, D. P. H. and Ranchandani, P. (1999) *Child Sexual Abuse*. Radcliffe Publishing, Oxford.

WEBSITES

www.everychildmatters.gov.uk/socialcare/integratedchildrenssystem
www.homeoffice.gov.uk
www.dh.gov.uk
www.wales.gov.uk
www.scotland.gov.uk

3 FACTORS CONTRIBUTING TO CHILD ABUSE AND NEGLECT

> ## This chapter covers:
> - **Theories**
> - **Social and environmental factors**
> - **Economic factors**
> - **Psychological factors**
> - **Genetic factors**
> - **Cultural differences in families**
> - **Predisposing factors**
> - **Domestic violence**
> - **The smacking debate**
> - **Disabled children**

Every occurrence of child abuse or neglect is part of a multifaceted past that leads to the current problem, something that may have begun years before the child was first harmed.

There are many factors that contribute to abusing and neglecting children. One thing is very clear: abuse is not restricted to any particular class, culture, race, religion or gender. In spite of this, many people have tried to build a picture of a perpetrator and the factors which may lead to abuse and neglect. It is unclear why some families are more vulnerable than others, and one needs to look at the whole context.

What has become obvious is that no professional or agency can work alone; we must work together as a community to identify, understand and prevent child abuse and neglect.

Theories concerning abuse

Over the past 50 years or so, many theories have been proposed to explain why some children are abused or neglected. One popular theory is based on the work that John Bowlby carried out on attachment. He worked at the Tavistock Clinic in London with James Robertson, who was looking at young children in hospitals and day nurseries who had been suddenly separated from their parents. Bowlby's work has been criticised as the research was retrospective and carried out on a specific small sample. The mothers of 44 juvenile thieves were questioned on their parenting and how they felt about their babies after the birth. Bonding is the term for the emotional attachment a mother feels for her newborn baby and the dependency of the baby on the mother. It was first used by Spitz in 1945 and made popular by John Bowlby in his 1958 paper for the World Health Organisation; more recently it has been used to include both parents.

Many theories place great emphasis on bonding

Other theorists interested in bonding include Mary Ainsworth in the 1970s and 1980s and more recently David Howe. In her 2004 book *Minding the Baby*, Sue Gerhardt points out the neurological connections that babies make when their stress responses receive adequate or inadequate responses, and the difference this makes to the relationships they form in later life. Responsive parenting enables the growing child to develop self-control and empathy and to feel connected to others.

It has been suggested that separating the mother from the baby immediately following the birth, for whatever reason, may interfere with the bonding process, so mothers are encouraged to touch and talk with their babies as soon as possible, even if the baby is in an incubator. Fathers are encouraged to be present at antenatal classes and at the birth, as this is thought to strengthen family relationships. In some cases of neglect and rejection, on looking back it is often apparent that, along with other negative factors, bonding did not happen satisfactorily. It would be foolish to conclude from this that the child is at risk if the bonding does not happen immediately, because in the vast majority of cases, the bonding takes place later on, as it does with adopted children.

Bowlby suggested that people who may have suffered from poor bonding and maternal deprivation as children are likely to have difficulty in acting as parents in later life, holding unrealistic expectations of their children and often resorting to ill-treatment. In many of the inquiries into the death of young children, the perpetrator was found to have been abused as a child. However, one should not necessarily conclude that all abused children go on to abuse as adults.

Another school of thought would suggest that inequalities within society such as poverty, poor housing, unemployment, lack of education, and lack of family and community support may lead to alienation, depression and poor parenting, but it has been shown that all types of abuse take place in all socio-economic groups.

Feminists might argue that a patriarchal society leads to abuse. Children are seen as possessions and are at the disposal of the male members of the household. However, it is clear that children are abused by women as well as men.

Sometimes one child in the family may be abused and treated as a scapegoat. There may appear to be no good reason for this, but it could be that the child is a stepchild, or has a disability or learning difficulties, or is perhaps a painful reminder of a past or present partner.

Current thought is that the reasons for child abuse must be looked at as a combination of social, psychological, economic and environmental factors. Abuse is found across a wider range of people than these individual theories would have us believe.

Social and environmental factors

The homes and lives of children in the UK have changed dramatically in the past 20 years. There are many possible reasons for this:

- increase in divorce and the number of households headed by one parent;
- increase in mobility, so that young families do not always have the support of an extended family, especially grandparents;
- increase in the number of reconstituted families (also known as 'merged' or 'restructured' families) and in the number of different relationships that the custodial parent might have;
- increase in stress due to unemployment, uncertainty in employment or longer hours in the workplace;
- increase in the number of children living in relative poverty;
- increase in drug and alcohol abuse;
- increase in violence on television, film and video/computer games;
- Easy access to computers, the internet and mobile phones;
- increase in reporting of violence in the media, leading to fear of children gaining independence outside the home and overshielding them from danger;

- increase in house-husbands or partners;
- increase in the involvement of the father in some aspects of child rearing;
- increase in the number of smaller families, so few children grow up with opportunities to learn about baby- and childcare through direct observation.

In some ways, the home has become a more claustrophobic place. Children do not have the freedom to play outside, even in their own gardens, and they spend more time in front of computers, televisions and videos.

Activity

Watch your favourite soap for two weeks. What issues are depicted that might be seen as indicators of the changes in our society? Look at a young child depicted in one of the soaps. If you were a childcare practitioner looking after that child, what factors in that family might you be concerned about?

Economic factors

Being poor does not in itself make parents more abusive, and most parents living in very deprived circumstances do not abuse or neglect their children, but the added stress that poverty brings may be a contributing factor. Lack of money means poor housing and fewer outings for the children, and the media shows a relatively affluent lifestyle as the norm.

The added stress that poverty brings may contribute to abuse or neglect

People who have a reasonable income are able to buy in domestic help and childcare support systems. Those with more money and easier access to higher education have a better understanding of how the system works and are able to take advantage of this. They are more aware of state entitlements and are more articulate in demanding help.

Lack of money can lead to an impoverished diet, inadequate clothing and poor health. Coping with frequent illness in children, or chronic illness in parents or children, leads to even more stress. Parents need to be in good health to cope with the demands of bringing up children.

Social workers, who can alleviate some of the stress of poverty by recommending day-care places and other services, are often unaware of problems in families who appear to be coping and do not seek help.

Those people who are well educated and have good job prospects are less likely to settle down in a relationship at a young age and may defer having children until they are financially stable. They are unlikely to experience unwanted pregnancies as they may well have a better understanding of contraception.

It is important to avoid stereotyping abusers as young, unmarried or poor, or drug or alcohol abusers, as these groups are much more open to scrutiny by social services and other professional workers than other groups.

To think about

Consider and discuss the following two statements: (1) government policies which allow children to grow up in poverty and deprived circumstances should be seen as a type of child abuse; (2) high unemployment levels in any society increase the incidence of child abuse.

CASE STUDY 3.1

Lewis is 4, small for his age and pale. He is disruptive and has a very short concentration span. His sister, Jade, is just 3 and is also small and pale with blonde wispy hair. They are both attending your nursery class and arrive in unsuitable dirty clothing, Jade in particular, smelling of urine. Their mother, Anita, is often drunk, even early in the mornings. She frequently complains of poverty and begs for money, stating she cannot feed the children. She arrived late one morning and threatened to cut her wrists in front of the children if some money was not forthcoming.

1 How do you respond to Anita'a threat?
2 What immediate help might you give the children?
3 What short-term help might be available for this family?
4 What long-term help might be found?

Providing nutritional school lunches can help the neglected child

Psychological factors

It could be the psychological make-up of one parent that leads to abuse or neglect. Psychological factors might include:

■ being brought up in a hostile family environment, so it is difficult to learn how to make loving relationships;

■ having excessive dependency needs, so a relationship will be kept going at any price, including domestic violence;

■ having a large number of children, in the hope that one will finally be the perfect child, while being unable to care properly for the needs of even one child;

■ having unrealistic expectations of children, not understanding their pattern of development and their limitations;

■ being excessively rigid and obsessive about routines, tidiness and the home environment while having little understanding of the chaos children can cause;

■ being unable to cope with stress;

■ being mentally ill;

■ being dependent on tranquillisers, drugs or alcohol;

■ experiencing closeness only after an episode of violence, which may relate to the adult's own childhood.

CASE STUDY 3.2

James is 3 and has been attending your nursery class for six months. The family are affluent, living in a large detached house. James's father is frequently away from home and James is usually collected from the class by an au pair. It has been difficult to establish a relationship with Felicity, James's mother. She seems to give him very little time or patience, often describing him in a disparaging manner. James is becoming quieter and more withdrawn and on one occasion describes being locked in a cupboard for what seemed like all day to him. When his mother arrives that day to collect him, she looks tearful, upset and unfocused. James runs and clings to his mother, who pushes him away.

1 What factors concern you?
2 How might his mother's rejection affect James's emotional development, and in what way might this threaten his later achievement at school?
3 What are James's needs and what are the family's needs?
4 What might you do to help James and his family?

Genetic factors

On 14 February 1997 Professor Emlen of Cornell University, in a controversial paper suggested that the decline of the nuclear family and the growth of single-parent and reconstituted families was linked to an increase in delinquency, truancy, child abuse and neglect. He suggested that although no gene for caring has yet been discovered, many species take more care of their immediate children because they have more of the same genes than strangers and unrelated children. Studies of birds and mammals, including humans, have shown that parents and grandparents tend to help their children effectively, protecting the genes that they have passed on to them. A number of contentious theories have been proposed which attempt to explain why relationships between parents and their biological children may be 'different' from those between carers and non-related children.

Activity
Identify any other theories you may have heard which try to explain inappropriate parenting.

Cultural differences in families

Families are unique in their attitudes to child-rearing practices. To some extent, the upbringing and history of the parents themselves plays a major part in the way their children are brought up. What might be thought of as encouraging independence in one family might be looked at as dangerous practice in another. Some parents are demonstrative and outgoing, whereas others are more restrained. The areas of difference are mainly:

- discipline and control;
- physical and emotional independence;
- providing a safe environment;
- diet, including attitudes to a fussy eater, providing an appropriate diet and using food as a reward or for comfort;
- attitude to education;
- provision of active play in or out of the home;
- mutilation of the body such as ear piercing, circumcision and tribal marks;
- attitude to nudity;
- employment of children;
- demonstrating affection;
- sleeping patterns, sharing beds or sharing rooms;
- tolerance of crying babies and children;
- attitude to noise made by children;
- ambitions for their children;
- relationship with their children;
- treating boys differently from girls;
- religion;
- moral guidelines.

To think about
It is thought by some that sexual abuse is found more often in families who are not open about sexual matters. Do you agree with this?

Activity
Some families allow their children more freedom and autonomy than others. List the advantages and disadvantages of allowing young children to make their own decisions.

Families show considerable variation in how they bring up children. Recognise the differences and do not leap to conclusions. Do not assume that certain religious or ethnic groups always behave in a particular fashion. These variations between and within families lead to the richness of today's diverse society.

Be non-judgemental and open-minded and avoid stereotyping, but if you consider that abuse is taking place in a family, you must challenge this, as the interests of the child are paramount.

Predisposing factors

It is very difficult to predict the circumstances in which abuse takes place; nevertheless, many researchers have suggested there may be some predisposing factors in individuals. These may relate to the adult's personality and background, problems in the adult's life and environment, and factors relating to the child. A combination of some of these factors is usually found in abusers:

- young parents reacting to situations in an immature manner, often lacking self-control and coping skills, perhaps poor parent–child interaction;
- parents who were abused themselves, who have a poor self-image, low self-esteem and poor parenting skills, and who may have unrealistic expectations of the child's abilities and developmental stages;
- family stress such as a crying baby, unemployment and chronic illness;
- inability to control anger;
- social isolation, with little back-up from the family or the community;
- substance abuse;
- reconstituted family;
- previous abuse, particularly if the original abuse was sadistic;
- separation after birth may be associated;
- learning difficulty and/or poor education;
- inability to enjoy life and experience pleasure;
- unsatisfactory social and personal relationships;
- fear of sparing the rod and spoiling the child;
- social problems such as poverty, poor housing and unemployment;
- the gender of the child;
- overwhelming personal problems, such as ill health and bereavement.

Activity
Which of the above factors might be found in all social classes?

To think about
We need to put more resources into researching the prevention of child abuse. Do you agree?

Becky, aged 3, has recently joined a nursery class. Her mother, Kristal, has a learning disability and is separated from Becky's father. Becky is a very energetic child, into everything, and Kristal is finding it very hard to manage her behaviour. She tends to keep her close and to stop her asking questions and exploring her environment. One day Becky arrives at the nursery with a large bruise on her arm. Kristal is very distressed and tells you that she has hit Becky.

1 What is your immediate reaction?
2 With whom should you discuss this?
3 How can you help and support Kristal?
4 How can the nursery help Becky?

THE VULNERABLE CHILD

The NSPCC has attributed vulnerability factors in child abuse and neglect to the child or to the parents.

Born too soon
- born before parents emotionally ready for the child;
- statistically more likely to have been born prematurely — weight lower and vulnerable to ill health; more difficult to handle and causes more anxiety.

Born sick or handicapped
- abnormal pregnancy, abnormal labour or delivery, neonatal separation, other separation in first six months, illness in first year of child and/or mother;
- difficult to feed — growth failure related to physical abuse, unsuccessful feeding may precipitate assault.

Born different
- parents' perception of difference is the one that is important.

Born unwanted
- unwanted pregnancy;
- unwanted gender;
- the child is a disappointing replacement for a lost child or someone precious.

THE VULNERABLE PARENTS

Unhappy childhood
- low self-esteem, more isolated, more life stresses, physical violence or fragile relationships;
- may expect criticism and rejection or resent authority.

TABLE 3.1 What Places Children "at risk" of Child Abuse?

The 'seven deadly sins': conditions and developmental stages that may trigger physical abuse of small children

Condition or trigger	Description	Age of most danger	Common abuse injuries associated	Advice for stopping abuse
Colic	All babies show some 'fussy' crying that is inconsolable. About 1 baby in 10 will cry like this frequently and persistently in ways parents find impossible to stop, and for long periods	1–3 months then stops	Internal bruising in head Grab-mark bruises Broken arms, legs and ribs	1 Check for any medical causes and then reassure parents this is normal and will stop at about 3 months or before 2 Help them to learn soothing techniques and give permission for them meeting their needs for sleep and time away from the baby
Habitual night crying	Some babies develop a habit of waking in the night even after they no longer need a feed. They get to enjoy the extra attention or find it difficult to sleep without parental care	4 months to 2–3 years	Internal bruising in head Grab-mark bruises Broken arms, legs and ribs	1 Stop naps during the day, move cot to baby's own room and make bedtime calm 2 Make 'check-up' visits short, boring and at long intervals 3 Give more attention and stimulation during the day
Clinginess and separation anxiety	At about 6 months a baby comes to depend upon his/her main caregiver(s) for security and will show clinginess and anxiety when separated. Some parents do not understand and see this as the child being spoiled	6 months to 3–4 years	Spanking and slapping injuries Emotional cruelty, e.g. locking up	1 Explain that this stage is normal and necessary for healthy development 2 Help parents to make separation easier for the child – by rehearsal, making it gradual, etc. 3 Make sure the child is always left with somebody they know, like and trust
Curiosity and exploration	Children as they develop mentally and physically increasingly explore their surroundings as they become more mobile. Unchecked they can expose themselves to danger. Some parents expect them to follow adult rules and punish them for damaging property or making messes	1–3 years	Too little control: burns, poisonings, etc. Too much control: bruised from spanking and rough grabbing	1 Explain that exploration and curiosity are natural and necessary parts of growing up 2 Safety-proof the home and draw up rules for protection, develop firm but non-abusive strategies for managing behaviour 3 Provide an environment that allows plenty of opportunities to explore
Disobedience and negativism	As children begin to develop a sense of independence, they often test this out by being disobedient and negative. Parents may feel very threatened by this disobedience	18 months to 3 years	Slaps and punches to body and head Cruel emotional punishment may include locking up, taunting, etc.	1 Explain that the phase is normal, however irritating 2 Go for minimal rules and non-confrontation 3 Offer the child choices where possible but don't bargain where there is no choice
Fussy eating	Because growth slows down, a child's appetite falls off somewhere between 18 months and 2 years. Refusing to eat may become a child's way of self-assertion	18 months to 3 years	Slap and pinch marks on face and injuries to mouth from force-feeding Children may choke or suffocate	1 Explain that it is usual to eat less at this age and reassure that the child is fit and well 2 Cut down on snacks and drinking too much milk 3 Take the 'heat' out of mealtimes
Wetting and soiling	Children gain control over their bladders and bowels only gradually. Parents may expect to toilet train too soon or see wetting and soiling as deliberate disobedience	1–3 years	Bruises, burns and scalds around bottom and genital areas	1 Advise parents to wait until the child is ready for toilet training 2 Don't attempt to train the child at times of stress 3 Be sympathetic about 'accidents'. They are very seldom deliberate

Early parenthood

■ youth and immaturity lead to unrealistic expectations of the child;
■ lack of practical knowledge;
■ child expected to meet parents' needs.

Psychological problems

■ no consistent pattern;
■ parents show psychiatric symptoms of stress at time of abuse;
■ attempted suicide of mother;
■ bereaved parents;
■ loss during pregnancy, may have relationship problems with newborn.

The table on page 43 shows some conditions and developmental stages of small children that may trigger abuse.

Domestic violence

Domestic violence features in over one-quarter of reported violent crimes in the UK, but many incidents will remain unreported. The majority of violence is inflicted by the male partner on the female partner. Some 43% of female murder victims (two a week) are killed by their present or former partner. About 100 000 women in London each week seek treatment for violent injuries caused by their partner or former partner.

The Women's Aid's Federation defines domestic violence as physical, sexual, psychological or financial violence that takes place within an intimate or family-type relationship that forms a pattern of coercive and controlling behaviour. Crime statistics and research show that domestic violence is gender specific (i.e. predominantly experienced by women and perpetrated by men) and that any woman can experience domestic violence regardless of race, ethnic or religious group, class, sexuality, disability or lifestyle. Children are often traumatised by witnessing domestic violence and are frequently abused by the same perpetrator who abuses their mother.

In 2003 the Department of Health acknowledged that 'At least 750 000 children a year witness domestic violence. Nearly three-quarters of children on the "at risk" register live in households where domestic violence occurs.'

Domestic violence and child abuse are inextricably linked. The central message of *Making an Impact*, a training pack launched in 1998 by the Department of Health, is that professionals working with children should be aware that domestic violence is an important indicator of risk of harm to children and that children are frequently abused by the same perpetrator as their mother.

In the UK, 23% of women aged 16–59 have been assaulted by their current or former partner. Children growing up with domestic violence are much more likely to experience child abuse and learn to accept violence as an appropriate method of resolving conflict.

The NSPCC has stated that alcohol is a factor in 40% of domestic violence incidents and 25% of known child abuse cases. In one London borough 40% of the children on the child protection register come from families where alcohol misuse is a serious problem.

Domestic violence is the second most common type of violent crime reported to the police and is found in all classes and cultures. Violent men often threaten to harm their children as a way of controlling their partners. In 90% of incidents, children were in the same room or a next-door room when violence took place.

To think about
Why do you think domestic violence is so seldom reported? Why do so many women remain in violent relationships?

It has been shown that short-term effects of this violence on the children included:

- problems at school;
- difficulty in making friends;
- emotional difficulties, such as withdrawal, aggression, displaying fear and anxiety.

The long-term effects included:

- lack of self-confidence;
- poor social skills;
- violent behaviour;
- depression;
- difficulties in forming relationships;
- disrupted education, so the child fails to reach its potential.

Many mothers were frightened about revealing the extent of the violence to anyone, through guilt and from fear that the children would be taken away. Many women who are the victims of domestic violence lack self-confidence and feel they are guilty of provoking the attacks. It has been recommended that all children living in violent situations must be considered 'children in need' under the Children Act. A social worker should assess their needs in order to offer support, counselling and therapy.

In 2003 the Barnardo's report *Bitter Legacy* confirmed earlier findings on how domestic violence affects children and young people. It also points out that children who witness domestic violence are made more vulnerable as adults and as young parents. Children who live within the shadow of domestic violence are often attacked and abused by the offender and without the example of a loving caregiver, they may go on to become abusers themselves.

The smacking debate

During the past decade there has been much debate on whether to smack children or not. The United Nations Committee on the Rights of the Child has twice recommended reform of UK legislation on the issue of smacking. In 1998 the

European Court of Human Rights ruled that British law does not provide adequate protection for children from assault by parents.

The protagonists line up on different sides. One side includes the Children Are Unbeatable! alliance. It has 350 organisations linked to its campaign, including the NSPCC, the National Children's Bureau, and Save the Children. All the major children's charities support the alliance's commitment to non-violence in parenting, childcare and education. The alliance will accept nothing less than a complete ban on smacking children. It does not support proposals to define 'acceptable ways of hitting children' as they are unworkable, unjust and increase the risk to children.

As long ago as 1995 the Gulbenkian Foundation report on children and violence proposed a national charter of non-violence. The chairman of the commission, Sir William Utting, was quoted as saying, 'Hitting people is wrong. Hitting children teaches them that violence is the most effective means of getting your own way. We must develop a culture which disapproves of all forms of violence. All the lessons of my working life point to the fact that violence breeds misery. It does not resolve it.'

The opposing arguments are often presented by parents who contend that smacking never did them any harm. They may quote the Bible, saying that if you spare the rod, you spoil the child. Many parents feel it would be an infringement of their parental rights to legislate against the way they choose to discipline their children and that a mild tap on the leg might lead to criminal proceedings. These parents would prefer a definition of 'reasonable chastisement' rather than complete prohibition.

The government's efforts to deal with this issue reflect increasing pressure to act, pressure from campaigners and from international institutions. There is a reluctance to totally prohibit smacking as they do not wish to be seen as a 'nanny state' and perhaps arouse parental hostility.

In July 1979 Sweden became the first country to ban all forms of corporal punishment of children by all carers, including parents. A report in February 2000 by Joan Durrant for Save the Children Fund showed that:

- youth crime rates did not rise;
- the proportion of youth convicted of theft declined by 21%;
- between 1970 and 1996 the proportion of youths involved in narcotics crimes declined by 75%;
- young people's drug and alcohol intake and suicide rates also declined;
- during the 1980s no Swedish child died as a result of physical abuse;
- four children were killed between 1990 and 1996 but only one at the hands of a parent;
- the number of children coming into care has decreased by 26% since 1982.

In the UK the picture is very different. In the 1990s the government commissioned researchers to interview parents and children in two-parent families in Britain. Here are three of its findings:

- almost half the children were hit weekly or more often;
- just over one-third had been punished severely;
- three-quarters of mothers stated that they had already smacked their baby before their first birthday.

Any change in legislation would be seen as an opportunity to educate parents about alternative methods of disciplining children, rather than as a way of prosecuting and punishing parents.

In 2002 the UK was condemned by the United Nations (UN) for continuing to permit the smacking of children 13 years after signing the UN Convention on the Rights of the Child. The UN report expressed 'deep regret' that Britain continues to tolerate 'the reasonable chastisement' of children by parents. Smacking constitutes 'a serious violation of the dignity of the child' and 'undermines the educational measures to promote positive and non-violent discipline'.

As a professional person looking after other people's children, it is never correct to administer physical punishment. There would never be any reason for a childcare practitioner to hit a child. You may find yourself in the position of explaining to parents the different acceptable methods of managing children's challenging behaviour.

To think about
Were you smacked as a child? If so, how did this affect you (a) in the short term and (b) in later life?

Activity
How might you manage the following situations?
- An older child deliberately provoking his younger brother into losing his temper and throwing food onto the floor.
- A child aged 3 refusing to go to bed, although obviously very tired.
- A child aged 3 wanting a bath rather than a shower, and refusing to cooperate.
- A child aged 6 taunting and teasing children from a different culture.
- A child demanding sweets in a busy supermarket.
- Three children quarrelling and fighting in a car.

Disabled children

Studies by Crosse and by Sullivan and Knutson have shown that disabled children are between two and four times more likely to be abused as other children. Disabled children are one of the most vulnerable groups in our society. They are often unable to speak up for themselves and can not communicate their experiences of abuse, but the trauma they suffer will be just as damaging for them as for any child.

The abuse and neglect of disabled children may include:
- force-feeding;
- segregation;

- discrimination;
- use of physical restraints;
- confinement to a room or to a bed;
- oversedation;
- lack of privacy;
- public toileting;
- isolation.

The abuse and neglect may arise from:

- stereotypes that exist in society;
- poor self-image and low self-esteem;
- passivity in their relationships due to lack of confidence and inability to assert themselves;
- communication difficulties;
- limited understanding of age-appropriate physical boundaries for children who require basic physical care;
- their need for love and affection, especially if they have experienced rejection.

Many child protection programmes do not include the disabled child, so they receive less information on how to protect themselves than other children. Safety programmes usually rely on a child's ability to understand the difference between appropriate and inappropriate touch. This is particularly true for the severely disabled who need help with all basic physical care. Perpetrators recognise their vulnerability, knowing that these children have difficulties in reporting abuse and in being believed.

When you start to work with children who are abused and with their families, it will become apparent that there are many factors contributing to the abuse or neglect. All cases are complex and some are never fully understood.

Every Child Matters is the Government agenda which focuses on bringing together services to support children and families. It sets out five major outcomes for all children:

- being healthy
- staying safe
- enjoying and achieving
- making a positive contribution
- economic well-being.

EVERY DISABLED CHILD MATTERS

Every Disabled Child Matters is a campaign to get rights and justice for every disabled child. It is jointly led by four organisations that work with disabled children and their families: Contact a Family, Council for Disabled Children, Mencap and the Special Educational Consortium. The organisation "will challenge politicians and policy-makers to make good on the Government's commitment that every child matters." Visit www.edcm.org.uk for further details.

Resources

Dwivedi, K. N. (2002) *Meeting the Needs of Ethnic Minority Children*. Jessica Kingsley, London.

Firth, L. (2007) *Child Abuse – Volume 132*, Independence Educational Publishers.

Gerhardt, S. (2004) *Why Love Matters: How Affection Shapes a Baby's Brain*. Routledge, London.

Howe, D. (1995) *Attachment Theory for Social Work Practice*. Palgrave, Basingstoke, Hants.

Howe, D. *et al.* (1999) *Attachment Theory, Child Maltreatment and Family Support: A Practice and Assessment Model*. Palgrave, Basingstoke, Hants.

Jackson, V. (1996) *Racism and Child Protection*. Cassell, London.

Kay, J. (2006) *Managing Behaviour in the Early Years*, Continuum.

WEBSITES

www.childrenareunbeatable.org.uk
www.childrenslegalcentre.com
www.nspcc.org.uk
www.rbkc.gov.uk
www.womensaid.org.uk

4. RECOGNISING ABUSE

> **This chapter covers:**
> - **Physical abuse and injury**
> - **Neglect**
> - **Emotional abuse**
> - **Sexual abuse**
> - **Failure to thrive**
> - **Organised abuse**
> - **Factitious illness**

Recognition of neglect and abuse is not easy; it is not your role as a childcare practitioner to decide whether or not abuse has taken place or if a child is at significant risk. You do have a responsibility to be aware of current child protection procedures and to report any concerns you may have to your line manager. You may become concerned:

- through observations you may record of a child;
- because of allegations made by a child or another person;
- because of disclosure of the abuse from a child or from the perpetrator.

In general, when a child has been abused, more than one type of abuse or neglect is present. If a child has been a victim of physical or sexual abuse, it is important to consider the emotional effect on the child's intellectual development and behaviour — the whole child needs to be considered. In this chapter we will outline the various signs of abuse and neglect separately, but you must always be conscious of possible overlap. It is also important for you to remember that, although the injury may not be accidental, it may not have been the intention of the parent or carer to harm the child, but may have resulted from different cultural approaches to discipline.

In this chapter we shall discuss many signs and indicators of abuse and neglect. You should always be cautious in your approach as sometimes there is an innocent explanation.

Physical abuse and injury

Physical abuse implies physically harmful action directed against a child. According to C. H. Kempe, it is usually defined by any inflicted injury such as bruises, burns, head injuries, fractures, abdominal injuries or poisoning.

Most children will suffer accidental injuries. It can be very difficult to decide what is accidental and what has been inflicted on a child, testing the skills of experienced paediatricians as many recent court cases have shown. Many signs which might lead you to suspect abuse may be explained in other ways. For example, bald patches may occur if children frequently twist and pull their hair as a comfort habit. Fractures may occur in some children with specific medical conditions. It is your responsibility to be alert to any unexplained or suspicious injury. Record your concerns, report them and discuss them with your line manager as soon as possible.

CASE STUDY 4.1

Chantal is 18 months old, she has an Afro-Caribbean father and an English mother, and she was routinely admitted to a workplace nursery. The newly qualified key worker, Zoë, identified what she thought were bruises on Chantal's buttocks and reported this to her experienced line manager, who examined the child and reassured the childcare practitioner that the marks were Mongolian blue spot, an area of natural hyperpigmentation that occurs in many African, Afro-Caribbean and Asian babies at birth.

1 Having read this chapter, can you identify any other signs or indicators that might be open to the wrong interpretation?
2 Do you think Zoë acted in a professional manner?

Physical signs

Injuries on the face, neck or head
■ All bruises on the head or face of a small baby should be investigated. Toddlers may fall and bruise themselves on the forehead, cheekbone or chin, but bruises on the cheek are suspicious, particularly if they appear on each side. Bruises may be caused by slapping, showing a distinctive outline. Punching a child results in an injury less defined, except if the child is punched in the ear or the eye, where distinctive bruising will be seen. Bruises on the scalp may be difficult to see but are tender to touch. Bruising of the lips and gums may be caused by hitting or ramming a feeding bottle into the mouth of a crying baby.
■ Bald patches may be seen on some children.
■ Cigarette burns, which may appear anywhere on the face or body, are small circular burns often seen at different stages, suggesting frequent and repeated incidents.
■ Small haemorrhages of the earlobe are rarely accidental. Two black eyes would be suspicious, especially if there is no other injury to the head or face. Haemorrhages in the eye can sometimes be seen, but are often invisible unless an ophthalmoscope is used. They can last for up to four weeks after the injury.
■ A direct blow to the head may fracture the skull. Shaking the child may lead

to bleeding in the head, sometimes resulting in a coma or convulsions. Severe injuries to the head may produce damage to nerves, leading to a squint.

- A torn frenulum (the tongue attachment) is suspicious, but may occur when a child contracts whooping cough, although this is extremely rare.
- Signs of injury on the neck should always be taken very seriously. This is a very rare site for accidental injury.
- Injuries to the limbs and torso.
- Fingertip bruising may be seen as a cluster of small bruises, like finger pressure marks often with the mark of the opposing thumb some distance away. This is seen where the child has been forcibly gripped, especially around the elbows and knees, on the trunk, and occasionally around the mouth. Thumb marks under the collarbones would indicate the child has been grasped and if on both sides, possibly shaken. Bruises on genitalia should always be regarded with great suspicion. Bruising anywhere on the body along a straight line would indicate being beaten with a belt, strap or stick. Bite marks will be seen as two semicircular bruises. Take care to distinguish between adult- and child-sized bites. Kicking a child results in diffuse bruising; occasionally there is a mark of the footwear. Bruises seen when the skin is close to a bone are usually accidental, but those on soft tissue such as the cheeks, mouth and buttocks are more suspicious. Bruises are seen in 90% of physically abused children. As they age, they change colour from red and blue, often swollen, to purple, to greenish brown and yellow.
- Small children, particularly babies, who are unable to move a limb, should have this injury investigated. Fractures may be caused by a direct blow to the limb or by grabbing and twisting the child's limb with some force.
- Scratches on the child's body may show fingernail marks.
- Injuries caused by scalds may be caused by dunking the child in very hot water, leaving a high water mark. Hot liquids thrown at a child may produce scattered splash burns. Hot liquid poured onto a child produces a broad linear mark. Marks on the soles of the feet might suggest 'dunking' a child on or near a fire. Burns on the buttocks are rarely accidental. Burns may also be caused by an iron or a hotplate, and these would show the telltale marks.

Some injuries are caused internally. Kicking or punching, injuring organs of the body such as liver, spleen or kidneys, can only be diagnosed by a doctor. Doctors investigating allegations of physical abuse will often call for a full skeletal X-ray. Children may also be physically abused by poisoning. This may be by medication, drugs, alcohol or other dangerous substances.

To think about
Child abuse may not be deliberate cruelty but something that happens when an adult loses control and cannot stop themselves. Do you think that an adult who deliberately abuses children is more at fault than an adult who loses control?

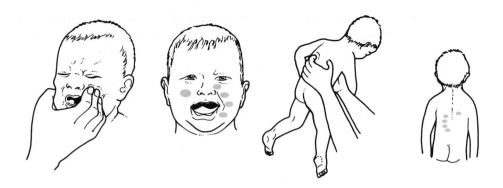

Fingertip bruising

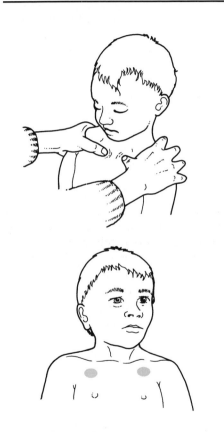

Thumb marks just below the collarbone

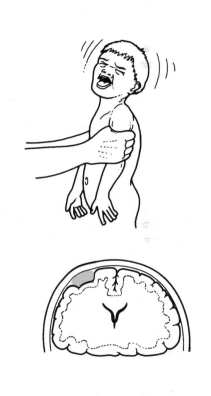

Subdural haematoma caused by rapid shaking of the head

Examples of fingertip bruising, thumb marks and shaking

CASE STUDY 4.2

Tracey, aged 4, has been happily settled in your nursery class for the past two terms. Her parents divorced one year ago but Tracey and her mother, Sandra, receive a great deal of support from her large extended family. One morning Tracey arrives with both eyes bruised, a bruise on her neck and a red mark on her ear. She tells you that she fell off her bike. An hour later, the maternal grandmother arrives, very agitated and saying that Sandra had phoned her in tears, saying that she had hit Tracey.

1 How do you react to this situation?
2 With whom do you discuss Tracey's injuries?
3 How do you respond to the grandmother?
4 What do you say to Sandra when she comes to collect Tracey?

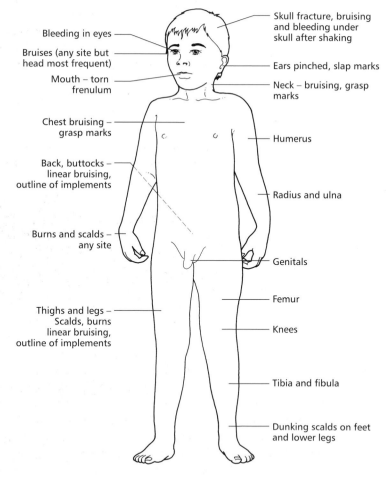

Bleeding in eyes

Bruises (any site but head most frequent)

Mouth – torn frenulum

Chest bruising – grasp marks

Back, buttocks – linear bruising, outline of implements

Burns and scalds – any site

Thighs and legs – Scalds, burns linear bruising, outline of implements

Skull fracture, bruising and bleeding under skull after shaking

Ears pinched, slap marks

Neck – bruising, grasp marks

Humerus

Radius and ulna

Genitals

Femur

Knees

Tibia and fibula

Dunking scalds on feet and lower legs

The principal injury sites

BEHAVIOURAL INDICATORS

Physical abuse may cause a change of behaviour in the abused child and a pattern of behaviour in the perpetrator. The behaviour in the child will obviously vary a great deal with the age of the child. The child may:

- withdraw from physical contact;
- withdraw from close relationships with adults and children;
- be apprehensive when other children cry;
- be frightened of parents or carers;
- fear returning home;
- show reluctance for the parents to be contacted;
- refuse to discuss the injury, or give improbable excuses;
- be reluctant to undress for PE or swimming or reluctant to remove clothes in hot weather;
- fear medical help or assistance;
- display frozen awareness: constant watchfulness of adults' reactions to them;
- display self-destructive behaviour;
- display aggression towards other children and adults;
- have a history of running away;
- show a change in eating pattern by refusing food or overeating.

If the perpetrator is the parent or carer, he or she may:

- keep the child at home for unexplained reasons;
- be unwilling to offer explanation for injuries;
- give unlikely excuses to explain injuries;
- fail to obtain treatment for injuries;
- hold extreme views on discipline and control.

Activity
List the needs of children to ensure optimum growth and development. Is it possible to list these in any order of priority?

Neglect

Neglect is the failure to provide minimum standards of care to meet the basic needs of children. It is the most prevalent form of child maltreatment and indicated in half the children on child protection registers in the UK. According to C. H. Kempe, neglect can be a very invidious form of abuse and can go on for a long time. It implies the failure of the parents to act properly in safeguarding the health, safety and well-being of the child. It includes nutritional neglect, failure to provide medical care or to protect a child from physical and social danger. We will look at neglect under three headings but they are often interrelated.

PHYSICAL NEGLECT

Signs of physical neglect
The child may be:

- underweight, small for their age, with poor muscle tone and a dry wrinkled skin;
- constantly hungry, found scavenging for food, displaying an enormous appetite if food is available, emaciated and may have a distended abdomen;
- dirty with their personal hygiene needs not being met, and may smell of urine; they will appear dirty and uncared for, with unbrushed hair and teeth; and clothing will be dirty and inappropriate for the time of year, possibly too large or too small;
- suffering from severe and persistent nappy rash and/or cradle cap;
- prone to frequent accidents through lack of supervision;
- constantly tired or lethargic;
- frequently unwell, with repeated colds and coughs, stomach upsets, and rashes; advice will not be sought for medical problems and they will remain untreated;
- frequently late for school or nursery; overall attendance will be poor.

Behavioural indicators
The child may display:

- low self-esteem and lack of confidence;
- neurotic behaviour such as rocking, hair twisting, headbanging and excessive masturbation;
- inability to make social relationships;
- destructive and aggressive tendencies;
- compulsive stealing, particularly of food;
- clinging behaviour to any adult.

EDUCATIONAL NEGLECT

A child who lacks stimulation from their home environment will find difficulty in achieving at school or nursery. Take care not to apportion blame to the parents as the neglect may have been unavoidable. For example, children from families fleeing from persecution in their own country may arrive in nurseries and schools with little experience of books, puzzles and games.

Signs and behavioural indicators of educational neglect
The child may display:

- poor language skills;
- low self-esteem and lack of confidence;
- developmental delay;
- short concentration span;
- limited experiences;
- inattention to a special educational need;
- unfamiliarity with books, stories and rhymes;
- unfamiliarity with jigsaws and construction toys, unused to any form of creative play;
- difficulty in expressing ideas and understanding new concepts.

CASE STUDY 4.3

You are working in the nursery class of a primary school and have been there for some time. Connor, aged 3, has just been enrolled in the class, following on from his three older siblings. The attendance of the family is known to be poor; sometimes several days go by without any of the children coming to school. Weak excuses are offered. If the children do come, they are usually late and are just pushed through the door. The sister in Year 6 takes the other children home at the end of the day, but this is rather late for Connor, who finishes the session half an hour earlier and waits in the staff room. The parents have never attended any parent–teacher meetings or participated in any social events.

1 Is there any way in which you can encourage the parents to bring Connor more regularly?
2 Are there any agencies that might be involved?
3 What strategies can you adopt to attempt to build a better relationship with the parents?

Activity
List three ways in which an infant school could help a child age 5 whose experiences of life outside the family were very limited?

EMOTIONAL NEGLECT

The parents may withdraw love from the child and fail to provide a home filled with warmth, interest and care. The parents often express unrealistic expectations in the behaviour of the child.

Signs and behavioural indicators of emotional neglect
The child may display:
- difficulty in making appropriate relationships with children and adults, and may be clinging or withdrawn;
- lack of discrimination in their attachment to an adult and may be over-friendly to all;
- fear of new situations;
- inability to express feelings;
- extreme comfort habits such as rocking, using a dummy or masturbating;
- low self-esteem and lack of confidence;
- unwillingness to take physical or intellectual risks.

In all forms of neglect, the adult may display:
- lack of responsibility, such as continually sending other people to collect the child from nursery or school, continually leaving the child unsupervised;
- lack of warmth;

- uncaring attitude;
- signs of stress;
- no interest in the child's progress or activities.

CASE STUDY 4.4

Orla is a small girl aged 2 years and 2 months. She is behind in her developmental progress and is not gaining in weight and height as one would expect. She has been in day care for four months and is the youngest of four children. Her mother is now a single parent; Orla's father left home shortly before her birth and has no further contact. She is often collected late and by different people. Orla is not an easy child to look after in the group; she is always demanding attention and is very clinging with adults. She is frightened of new situations. She enjoys her food and eats well in the nursery, usually asking for second helpings.

1 Do you think there is cause for concern? Why?
2 What observations might help you find out more about her situation?
3 What records should you maintain for this child and her family?
4 How might you improve your communication with the mother?
5 Are there any special activities you might devise to help Orla with her social behaviour?

Emotional abuse

According to C. H. Kempe, 'Emotional abuse includes a child being continually terrorised, berated, or rejected.' A child who is brought up in a home where there is little or inconsistent love or warmth will find it difficult to respond appropriately to their own or other people's emotional needs. This is even truer of children who are continually and repetitively bullied, made scapegoats and told that they are stupid and a failure or are constantly ridiculed, shouted at and undermined. Emotional abuse is the most complex form of abuse to recognise and is often seen as a secondary feature of other forms of abuse.

Signs and behavioural indicators of emotional abuse
The child may display:
- fear of new situations
- comfort-seeking behaviour
- speech disorders such as stammering and stuttering
- all-round developmental delay
- inappropriate emotional responses
- inability to cope with making errors
- extremes of passivity or aggression
- fear of parents being contacted

- low self-esteem and lack of confidence
- self-mutilation by head-banging, pulling out hair and picking at skin
- poor concentration span
- stealing and telling lies
- wetting and soiling after the age you would expect a child to be clean and dry
- attention-seeking behaviour
- inability to have fun
- poor social relationships
- temper tantrums which are not age-appropriate.

An adult who is an emotional abuser may:

- show dislike or rejection of the child
- have a history of neglect and abuse themselves
- be locked in conflict with a partner
- be mentally ill
- be abusing drugs or alcohol
- have very unrealistic behavioural or academic expectations of the child
- have a psychopathic personality
- punish harshly or in a bizarre way
- swing between indulgence and harsh discipline and be unpredictable.

To think about

Policies concerning child abuse need to (a) strike a balance between protecting children and respecting family privacy and (b) be antidiscriminatory and culturally aware. What difficulties might there be in achieving this?

Sexual abuse

Working Together to Safeguard Children defines sexual abuse like this: 'Forcing or enticing a child or young person to take part in sexual activities whether or not the child is aware of what is happening. The activities may involve physical contact, including penetrative (e.g. rape or buggery) or non-penetrative acts. They may include non-contact activities, such as involving children in looking at pornographic material or watching sexual activities, or encouraging children to behave in sexually inappropriate ways.'

It is a betrayal of trust and responsibility and an abuse of power that allows the perpetrator to coerce a child to take part in sexual activity. Sexual abuse happens to boys and girls, and is perpetrated by both men and women. It ranges from showing children pornographic material or touching them inappropriately to penetration, rape and incest. It is found in all cultures and in all classes of society, in all types of families and across all religious groups. It can start with newborn babies.

The majority of abused children know the perpetrator, who is often a member of the family, a close friend or someone in a position of trust. Any act committed by a stranger would be considered sexual assault rather than sexual abuse and would be handled by the police and criminal courts. In very young children, because they trust the loved adult, it may take some years before they realise that the abuse does not happen to everyone. They may feel it is wrong, but have no experience to compare it with.

To think about
The medical diagnosis of child abuse should never be based on the assessment of just one doctor. Do you agree? Why?

More than any other form of abuse, sexual abuse within the family is a way of displaying power. It rarely involves the use of physical force, as children are trusting and dependent. They want to please and gain love and approval. They believe that adults are always right. The abuse often begins gradually and increases over time. It is a violation of a child's right to a normal, healthy, trusting relationship and often causes them difficulty in making satisfactory sexual relationships when they become an adult.

Physical signs of sexual abuse or assault
- sustain bruises, scratches or bites to the genital and anal area, chest, neck or abdomen
- have bloodstained or torn underclothing
- show semen on the skin or clothing
- complain of soreness or discomfort in the anal or vaginal areas, or in the throat
- complain of common ailments, such as stomach pains or headaches
- cry hysterical when the napkin or clothing is removed
- display bleeding in the throat, anal or vaginal areas
- experience discomfort when walking or sitting
- experience pain when urinating.

Boys may complain of:
- a swollen penis
- discharge from the penis.

Girls may complain of:
- vaginal discharge.

If referred to a paediatrician, the following may be detected:
- sexually transmitted disease
- semen in the vagina or anus
- internal small cuts in the vagina or anus
- abnormal swelling (dilation) of the vagina or anus
- thrush and urinary tract infections
- pregnancy.

Behavioural indicators of sexual abuse or assault

Quite often, there are no physical indicators of abuse, and the recognition of behavioural indicators becomes crucial.

The child may:

- show fear of a particular person
- regress developmentally
- display insecurity and cling to parents
- behave in a way sexually inappropriate to his or her age, showing an obsession with sexual matters, particularly in doll and role play
- produce drawings of sex organs, such as erect penises and huge breasts
- display withdrawn, sad behaviour and appear unhappy and confused
- demonstrate variations in appetite, perhaps leading to an eating disorder
- demonstrate poor concentration
- show a change in sleeping habits, becoming wakeful or complaining of chronic nightmares
- begin wetting again when previously dry
- act in a placatory or flirtatious way, or in an inappropriately mature way
- be unable to sustain social relationships with other children
- show a range of unpredictable behaviour from withdrawn and fearful to aggressive and hurtful
- introduce obscene words into their language
- display low self-esteem and lack confidence.

Young children will often display many of these behavioural traits at one time or another without them being indicators of sexual abuse. Warning bells should ring if these persist for long periods, or if many of them happen again.

As children develop their language and independence, you may become aware of other behavioural indicators. The child may:

- start to drop hints about secrets
- ask if you can keep secrets
- talk about 'a friend's' problem
- tell lies
- bathe excessively or have poor personal hygiene
- display phobic or panic attacks
- steal or cheat, perhaps in the hope of being caught
- have unexplained amounts of money
- be reluctant to undress for games, swimming or PE
- be reluctant to join in outside activities
- refuse to see or express dislike of certain people
- develop eating disorders, such as anorexia or bulimia
- become severely depressed
- display poor self-image, frequently describing him or herself as dirty, evil or wicked
- attempt to run away from home.

CASE STUDY 4.5

Leanne, aged 4, has been attending a nursery class for 12 months. One morning she complains of having a sore bottom and when taken to the lavatory the childcare practitioner notices bloodstains on her pants. Leanne says that Scott, her mother's boyfriend for the past two months, 'pokes' her bottom. She says she does not like Scott as he gets angry if she is unwilling to 'play the game'.

1 How should you respond to this?
2 Do you think Leanne is being abused? What type or types of abuse?
3 What other indicators would you look for?
4 What might be the likely physical, emotional and educational effects on a child in the short term and in the long term?
5 What are Leanne's immediate needs in this situation?
6 What are the needs of the family?

FEMALE SEXUAL ABUSERS

During the 1990s there was a growing awareness that men are not the only sexual abusers of young children. Michele Elliott, director of Kidscape, wrote in *Social Work Today* (12 March 1992) that, following her appearance to discuss female abusers on a local radio phone-in, 100 people contacted her to say they had been abused by a female, frequently acting alone and not under the influence of a male partner.

Activity
Women appear to have become more assertive and aggressive during the past decade. Identify positive and negative effects of this development.

There are few statistics showing how much sexual abuse is perpetrated by women. This may be because:
- The concept of women as abusers is threatening, as women are perceived as nurturing caregivers, the natural protectors of children.
- Women are not supposed to be sexually aggressive.
- People who have disclosed have not been believed and have been told that they are fantasising.
- People find it difficult to understand that a woman could sexually abuse a child.

Thirty years ago, sexual abuse of young children by either sex was thought to be extremely rare. The media and ChildLine have raised the awareness of the general public and it is now accepted that sexual abuse by females is more prevalent than previously thought.

Failure to thrive

Children who are abused are often diagnosed as 'failing to thrive'. This refers to children who fail to grow in the expected way, for no organic or genetic reason. Obtain a clear medical history of the child so you can rule out organic factors such as malabsorption of nutrients, infection and major illness. Other children will fail to thrive because of stress, poverty or poor parenting. Poor parenting may be linked with neglect but it need not be deliberate. All children who fail to thrive should be referred to a paediatrician. Percentile growth charts may be used to assess and monitor the child's growth, head circumference and height in addition to other investigations. Many infants may cross up or down one or two percentiles, particularly in the first year. Children who are failing to thrive because of abuse or neglect will often start to gain weight and grow if removed from the family home for a period of time.

CASE STUDY 4.6

Aimee, aged 2 years, and her sister Mia, aged 6 months, have just been admitted to your day nursery on the recommendation of their health visitor. Aimee has 'failed to thrive' and is being seen by the paediatrician at the local hospital. When you lift Mia out of the pram you notice maggots crawling under the mattress.

1 What is your immediate course of action?
2 How might you help the children in the long term?
3 What agencies would be involved in supporting this family?

PAEDIATRIC ASSESSMENT

A child may be referred to a paediatrician for an opinion on the medical aspects of abuse and/or neglect. The paediatric assessment should:
- confirm the suspicion of any abuse or neglect;
- contribute to any child protection inquiries;
- give evidence for any care or criminal proceedings, if appropriate;
- identify any medical problems that may cause the symptoms or signs of abuse or neglect;
- inform and reassure the child and the family of any consequences of any injury;
- lead to the provision of follow-up medical support and treatment;
- lead to monitoring of any improvement or deterioration in the child's health;
- consider the safety and welfare of any siblings and their need for assessment.

Organised abuse

The physical signs and behavioural indicators of organised abuse have already been described under sexual and emotional abuse. This type of abuse is often associated with bizarre sadistic behaviour arousing extreme terror in the victims. The existence of this type of abuse is often debated, but the fear of the victims makes disclosure very difficult, so it is often impossible to collect objective evidence.

Factitious illness

Factitious illness, sometimes known as Munchausen syndrome by proxy, is a rare and severe personality disorder usually found in women, create the symptoms of disease in the child. It usually involves mothers who are very closely bonded to their children and who tend to have detailed medical knowledge. The symptoms are real and convincing; they may range from putting blood on a child's nappy or in a urine sample to giving laxatives that cause diarrhoea. This may be followed by inappropriate and painful tests in hospital, or even submitting the child to an operation.

A woman who creates the symptoms of disease in her child is suffering from factitious illness

There have been cases where dangerous drugs or poisonous substances have been administered to the child while under observation in hospital. It is difficult to diagnose the condition as the mother often appears very attentive and concerned, and may form close relationships with the hospital staff.

Childcare practitioners should be concerned if a seemingly healthy child is being constantly admitted to hospital. Other warning signs might be:

- The illness is unusual, prolonged and affects different parts of the body.
- The symptoms are inappropriate and do not seem to fit the illness.
- The child has multiple allergies.
- The symptoms disappear when the parent or carer is absent.
- There is only one parent present during hospitalisation.
- There is a history of sudden infant death syndrome in the family.
- The parent is overly attached to the child.
- The parent shows inordinate concern for the feelings of the medical staff.

GOOD PRACTICE

In recognising abuse:
1 Be alert to all signs of abuse, but be careful not to jump to conclusions; many of the signs can be put down to other causes.
2 Keep up to date and have a good knowledge of developmental norms and age-appropriate behaviour.
3 Remember that abuse occurs in all strata of society and in all cultures and religions.
4 If you suspect abuse, be discreet; discuss your suspicions only with your line manager.
5 Your role is to observe, record and report suspected abuse, not to investigate it. Make notes immediately and record exactly what the child says and does. Do not add your own interpretation of the child's words. All notes should be signed and dated then kept in a safe place.
6 Be very tactful and sensitive in the way you touch and communicate with a child whom you suspect has been abused.
7 Remember that an abused child will generally have experienced more than one kind of abuse.
8 Do not question the child again once disclosure has taken place, as you may influence legal proceedings and increase the child's anxiety and distress.

As a childcare practitioner in daily contact with young children, you have developed sensitive and accurate observation skills and have a sound knowledge of children's developmental progress. This makes you the professional most likely to recognise signs and behavioural indicators of abuse.

KEY TERMS

You need to know what these words and phrases mean:

accidental injury
behavioural indicators
developmental delay
development of the whole child
female sexual abusers
fingertip bruising
frozen awareness
inflicted injury
informed consent
low self-esteem
perpetrator
sexual assault
social taboos

Resources

Beckett, C. (2007) *Child Protection: An Introduction*, 2nd edn. Sage, London.

Corby, B. (2005) *Child Abuse: Towards a Knowledge Base*, 3rd edn. Oxford University Press, Oxford.

Elliott, M. (1996) *Female Sexual Abuse of Children: The Ultimate Taboo*, Pitman, London.

Hewitt, S. K. (1999) *Assessing Allegations of Sexual Abuse in Pre-school Children*. Sage, London.

Horwath, J. (ed.) (2001) *The Child's World: Assessing Children in Need*, Jessica Kingsley, London.

Horwath, J. and Lawson, B. (eds) (1995) *Trust Betrayed: Munchausen Syndrome by Proxy*, National Children's Bureau, London.

Iwaniec, D. (2006) *The Emotionally Abused and Neglected Child*, 2nd edn. Wiley, Chichester, W. Sussex.

NSPCC (2008) *Protecting Children from Sexual Abuse: a Guide for parents and carers*, NSPCC Publications, London.

O'Hagan, K. (2006) *Identifying Emotional and Psychological Abuse*, Oxford University Press, Oxford.

5 THE RIGHTS OF CHILDREN AND THE LEGAL FRAMEWORK

This chapter covers:
- **The rights of children**
- **The Children Act 1989**
- **Child protection orders**
- **The Data Protection Act 1998**
- **The Sexual Offences Act 2003**
- **Going to court**
- **Local procedures**
- **Referrals and investigations**
- **The child protection conference**
- **The child protection register**
- **Reviews and deregistration**

To play an effective part in protecting children in your care, you need to have a clear understanding of the rights of children, the legal framework, and the national and local guidelines published for all professionals working with children. Common law has long required any person looking after a child to protect them from physical harm by providing the necessities of life, based on need. Statutory responsibility for child protection rests with the social services department of the local authority.

Activity
Identify some countries where currently it would not be possible to implement all children's rights. What factors are usually present?

The rights of children

In November 1959 the United Nations (UN) issued a document declaring the rights of the child. This was motivated by the plight of some children due to wars and famine: children left without parents, families and homes. The following rights are set out:
- the right to equality, regardless of race, colour, religion, sex or nationality;
- the right to healthy mental and physical development;
- the right to a name and a nationality;
- the right to sufficient food, housing and medical care;
- the right to special care, if handicapped;
- the right to love, understanding and care;

- the right to free education, play and recreation;
- the right to medical aid in the event of disasters and emergencies;
- the right to protection from cruelty, neglect and exploitation;
- the right to protection from persecution and to an upbringing in the spirit of worldwide brotherhood and peace.

Thirty years later, in 1989, the convention was adopted and further points were added. Applicable to child protection was the statement that it is: 'the right of every child to a standard of living adequate for the child's physical, mental, spiritual, moral and social development'.

The convention contains more than 30 articles incorporating civil, economic, social and cultural rights. Article 3, the welfare principle, states that 'in all actions concerning children, whether undertaken by public or private social welfare institutions, courts of law, administrative authorities or legislative bodies, the best interests of the child shall be a primary consideration'.

Article 19 defines protection from abuse. It aims to protect the child from 'all forms of physical or mental violence, injury or abuse, neglect or negligent treatment, maltreatment or exploitation including sexual abuse while in the care of parent/s, legal guardian/s or any other person who has the care of the child'.

Protective measures include support for the child and identification, reporting, referral, investigation, treatment, and follow-up of instances of child maltreatment. Article 34 concerns protecting the child from sexual abuse and sexual exploitation. This is defined as:

- inducement or coercion of a child to engage in any unlawful sexual activity;
- exploitative use of children in prostitution or other unlawful sexual practices;
- exploitative use of children in pornographic performances and materials.

It is clear that in many countries it would be impossible to grant all these rights, as even the basic needs for food and shelter cannot be met. But the convention is an important document because it recognises the rights of children who have been abused. We need to understand the rights of children and respect them.

In 1990 the National Children's Bureau (NCB) set out a policy for young children, in particular the under-5s. The principles of this policy are that:

- Young children are important in their own right and as a resource for the future.
- Young children are valued and their full development is possible only if they live in an environment which reflects and respects their individual identity, culture and heritage.
- Parents are primarily responsible for nurturing and supporting the development of their children and that this important role should be more highly valued in society.
- Central and local government have a duty, working in partnership with parents, to ensure that services and support are available for families: services that encourage children's cognitive, social, emotional and physical development; and meet parents' needs for support for themselves and for day care for their children.

- Services for young children should be provided within a consistent legal framework which allows for flexibility but which ensures basic protection against pain and abuse, equal opportunities and the absence of discrimination, and development of the child as an individual through good quality childcare practice.

GOOD PRACTICE

Explain to children that they have rights:
1   Teach children that everyone has rights which should not be taken away, such as the right to be safe.
2   Teach children that their bodies belong to them and no one else.
3   Teach children the right to say no to any touching they do not like. This needs teaching, as children are generally brought up to be obedient and polite to adults.

The Human Rights Act 1998 came into force in the UK in 2000 and reflects the European Convention on Human Rights. The Act confers the same rights on children as it does on adults, as being in their own right capable of taking part in decision making about their futures. Any judgements concerning human rights are often a balance. For example, in 2001 the European Court of Human Rights ruled against Newham Council in London for wrongly taking a child into care in breach of Article 8 of the Human Rights Convention, which enshrines respect for family life. On the same day, the European Court decided unanimously that the failure by Bedfordshire Social Services to intervene for almost five years to protect four brothers and sisters from abuse by their parents amounted to violation of Article 3 of the convention, which prohibits degrading and inhuman treatment.

Children Act 1989

The Children Act 1989 came into force on 14 October 1991. It has had a major impact on the law relating to children, affecting all children and their families. Much of the old law was abolished and the emphasis of the new law was that parents should have responsibilities for their children, rather than rights over them. Parental responsibility is defined as the rights, duties, powers, responsibilities and authority that, by law, a parent of a child has in relation to the child and to their property.

The Children Act acknowledged the importance of the wishes of the child. Parental rights diminish as the child matures. Parental responsibility is an important concept when deciding who is in a position to make decisions about the child, and who should be contacted in any legal proceedings. Those who can hold parental responsibility are:

- *The mother*, who always has it, whether married or not. She can only lose it when an adoption or freeing order is made.
- *The natural father*, who has it jointly with the natural mother if they are married to each other at the time of the child's birth, or subsequently marry. He can only lose it if an adoption or freeing order is made.
- *The unmarried father*, who may acquire it by agreement with the mother or by court order.
- *The step-parent* can acquire it by obtaining a residence order and will lose it if that order ends.
- *The local authority* acquires it when obtaining a care order or emergency protection order and loses it when that order ends.
- *Others*, such as grandparents, may acquire it by court order and will lose it when the order ends.

Activity
Obtain a copy of the Children Act 1989 or *An Introduction to the Children Act 1989*, which is easier to read. Make a note of all the sections which refer primarily to child protection.

Parental responsibility may not be surrendered or transferred. It can be shared with a number of persons and/or the local authority. Each individual having parental responsibility may act alone in exercising it, but not in a way that is incompatible with any court order made under the 1989 Act. The Act sets out a series of principles dictating practice and procedure in and out of court. The key messages of the Act are shown below.

Section 17 of the Children Act states that it is the duty of every local authority to safeguard and promote the welfare of children within their area who are in need, and attempt to promote the upbringing of such children by their families by providing a range and level of services appropriate to those children's needs.

THE CHILDREN ACT 1989

PRINCIPLES OF THE ACT

- Children are generally best looked after within their families.
- Parents and guardians retain parental responsibility and work in partnership with the local authority.
- No court order to be made unless better than making no order at all.
- The child's welfare is the court's paramount consideration.
- The local authority cannot acquire parental responsibility without a court order.
- Orders available to protect children and avoid unwarranted intervention in family life.

DUTIES AND POWERS

- Identify children in need, safeguard and promote their welfare within their families where consistent.
- Provide a range and level of appropriate services.
- Consult child, parent, those with parental responsibility and others whom the agency considers relevant when making decisions about the child.
- Have regard to child's race, religion, culture and language when making decisions about children being looked after.
- Set up representations and complaints procedure and publish its existence.
- Use orders under Parts IV and V if child is suffering or likely to suffer significant harm.

PRINCIPLES AND PRACTICE GUIDE

- Children, young people and their parents should be considered as individuals with particular needs and potential.
- A child's age, sex, health, personality, race, culture and life experiences are all relevant to any consideration of needs and vulnerability and have to be taken into account when planning or providing help.
- There are unique advantages for children in experiencing normal family life in their own birth family and every effort should be made to preserve the child's home and family links.

- The development of a working partnership with parents is usually the most effective route to providing supplementary or substitute care for their children.
- The wishes of the children should be taken into account. Children should be consulted and kept informed.
- Decisions made in court should be responsive to the needs of children, promote their welfare and reached without undue delay.
- Where children are placed away from home there must be adequate supervision that ensures highest-quality substitute parenting with good standards of care and safety.
- Parents' contact with children should be maintained wherever possible.

EQUALITY ISSUES

- Attitudes towards 'the family': the influence of institutional, societal and personal belief and experience on assessment and planning.
- Skills and knowledge available to accurately consult with the child, relatives and others.
- Ability to take into account the factors of race, culture, language and religion.
- Ability to understand the effect of disability on the whole family. Parents should be helped to raise the children themselves.
- Openness to working in partnership; developing a combination of antidiscriminatory policies; commitment to guaranteed resource provision; support to enable staff to work with confidence.

Activity
- What factors might contribute to families being wrongly suspected of child abuse?
- As a childcare practitioner working in a socially deprived area, how might you contribute to reducing the stress felt by families?

To think about
Discuss with your group:

- Women from cultures where male children are valued should have free access to termination of female foetuses.
- Women undergoing in vitro fertilisation (IVF) treatment should be allowed to choose the gender of their unborn children.

The 1989 Act required local authorities to set up Area Child Protection Committees (ACPCs) consisting of professionals representing all the agencies involved in caring for children, such as social services, education, police, probation services, health services and voluntary organisations. The Department of Health document *Working Together to Safeguard Children* outlined the following responsibilities of an ACPC:

- To develop and agree local policies and procedures for interagency work to protect children.
- To audit and evaluate how well local services work together.
- To put in place objectives and performance indicators for child protection.
- To encourage and develop good working relationships between different services and professional groups based on trust and mutual understanding.
- To ensure there is a level of agreement and understanding across agencies about operational definitions and thresholds for intervention.
- To improve local ways of working in the light of knowledge gained through national and local experience and research, and to make sure that any lessons learned are shared, understood and acted on.
- To undertake case reviews where a child has died or in certain cases been seriously harmed and abuse or neglect are confirmed or suspected.
- To communicate clearly to individual services and professional groups their shared responsibility for protecting children and to explain how each can contribute.
- To help improve the quality of child protection work through delivering training.
- To raise awareness.

Following concerns that some ACPCs were not working well in some areas because of the low priority given to safeguarding children by some of them, resulting in lack of resources for child protection and lack of senior management commitment, the Children Act 2004 stated that local authorities have a duty to set up Local Safeguarding Children Boards (LSCBs). These consist of representatives from all agencies and coordinate the functions of all agencies in relation to safeguarding children. They replace the ACPCs and should be chaired by the director of children's services, taking on all the responsibilities listed above, plus they can commission independent serious case reviews and manage a service to look at unexpected child deaths.

Child protection orders

Since implementation of the Children Act 1989, many children at risk of harm can be satisfactorily protected without going to the courts. Where this is not possible, the Act introduced new child protection orders.

A CHILD ASSESSMENT ORDER

A child assessment order may be applied for only in court, on notice by a local authority or the NSPCC. It is used when there is reasonable cause to believe that a child is suffering or is likely to suffer significant harm and it would be very difficult to obtain a satisfactory assessment of the child's health and development without such an order. The order lasts for a maximum of seven days.

AN EMERGENCY PROTECTION ORDER

An emergency protection order is intended for use only in real emergencies and enables a child to be made safe when they might otherwise suffer harm. The order lasts for a maximum of eight days and can be extended once only for a further seven days. Anyone can apply to the court for this emergency order. While it is in force the local authority will have limited parental responsibility. It may set out who may be allowed or refused contact with the child. It may involve assessment of the child.

A RECOVERY ORDER

Recovery orders apply to children in care following an emergency protection order or children in police protection. If such a child is missing, has been abducted or has run away from the person responsible for their care, the court may make a recovery order and this will be implemented by the police.

> **To think about**
> Policies concerning child abuse are not always effective. How could they be improved?

A SUPERVISION ORDER

A supervision order will be applied for by the local authority if it has been unable to make satisfactory voluntary arrangements with the parents to ensure the child's protection. The child is placed under the supervision of the local authority. The local authority does not have parental responsibility but does have rights of access to the child to ensure the child's well-being. The order can last up to one year and can be extended.

This should not be confused with another type of supervision order with the same name, which is a community sentence given to young offenders by the youth court under the Crime and Disorder Act 1998. It requires the offender to be "supervised" by an appropriate person, often a member of the Youth Offending Team.

> **Activity**
> Discuss with your placement supervisor how to find a copy of local procedures. Which agencies will be involved?

A CARE ORDER

A care order places the child in the care of the local authority. It does not necessarily mean that the child is away from home, but the parental responsibility is shared by the local authority and the parents. In any dispute over the arrangements for the child, the local authority would have the final say. The local authority has the power to remove the child from home without applying for any other order. The care order lasts until the child is 18 unless the court discharges the order earlier. The police also have separate powers to protect children, lasting up to 72 hours. An Interim Care Order can also be made. It has the same effect as a full Care Order while it lasts. The first Interim Care Order can last for up to 8 weeks. It can then be renewed for up to 28 days at a time. An unlimited number of interim care orders can be made. The police also have separate powers to protect children, lasting up to 72 hours. During this time the designated police officer may apply for an emergency protection order.

Data Protection Act 1998

The Data Protection Act 1998 regulates the handling of information kept about an individual on a computer or in a manual filing system. The Act requires that personal information is:

- accurate and relevant;
- kept secure;
- obtained and processed fairly and lawfully;
- processed for limited purposes and not in any manner incompatible with those purposes;
- held for no longer than necessary;
- only disclosed if specific conditions set out in the Act are satisfied.

Government guidance issued in May 2003 confirmed that disclosure of information should not be an obstacle if an individual has particular concerns about the welfare of a child, the information is disclosed to another professional and disclosure is justified under the common law duty of confidence. The Information Commissioner's Office (ICO) is the UK's independent authority set up to promote access to official information and to protect personal information. Full Data Protection Guidelines are given on their website at www.ico.gov.uk.

Sexual Offences Act 2003

The aim of the Sexual Offences Act 2003 is to protect the safety and rights of young people and make it easier to prosecute people who pressure or force others into having sex they do not want. The Act includes:

- new laws designed to tackle all inappropriate sexual activity with children, including causing a child to engage in sexual activity;
- a civil order to apply on the Internet and offline, which will enable restrictions to

be placed on people displaying inappropriate sexual behaviour towards a child before an offence is committed;

- increased penalties for sexual crimes against children to reflect the severity of these crimes;
- an automatic charge of rape which carries a maximum life sentence for sex with 12-year-olds and under;
- a new grooming offence with a maximum sentence of 10 years;
- the requirement that all registered sex offenders confirm their details in person annually;
- a new offence of trafficking people for sexual exploitation;
- a new order to make sex offenders from overseas register as offenders when they come to the UK;
- the definition of rape extended to include penetration of the mouth by the penis.

Under this law the legal age for young people (straight, gay or bisexual) to consent to have sex is still 16. Young people under 16 still have the right to confidential advice on contraception, pregnancy and abortion.

Going to court

If there is a decision to go to court, this should be planned as carefully as possible. The decision is taken by the local authority, usually after consultation with other agencies, and after taking advice from their law departments. The process will start

Childcare practitioners may be asked to give evidence in court

in the local family proceedings court (the magistrates' court). When applying to the courts, the application must clearly identify the grounds for concern, and the proposed medium- and long-term future plans for the child.

If, as a childcare practitioner, you are called to act as a witness by the local authority, you are entitled to legal advice concerning your evidence from the local authority lawyer. If there is a conflict between you and the local authority, you must ask your own employer to provide legal advice from another lawyer, experienced in childcare proceedings.

As a general rule, all professionals have a responsibility to disclose information to other relevant agencies where there is any suspicion that a child is being abused. It is important not to share this information with any other person or agency, as it may leave you open to legal action. Any record may be subpoenaed by the courts for either civil or criminal proceedings. There are rules governing disclosure of documentation and confidentiality in court proceedings, and you should always obtain legal advice in these situations.

To think about
You think a child might be being abused in the block of flats where you live. You have not witnessed any abuse, but are highly suspicious as the 3-year-old in the family always looks unhappy and neglected. What should you do? What range of feelings might you experience?

Local procedures

All child protection services are built around the following documents:
- *Working Together to Safeguard Children: A guide to inter-agency working to safeguard and promote the welfare of children*, 2006, Every Child Matters;
- *Framework for the Assessment of Children in Need and Their Families*, published by the Department of Health in 2000;
- *What to Do if You're Worried a Child is Being Abused*, Every Child Matters.

The LSCBs, established by the Children Act 2004, are then expected to define in more detail the procedures to be followed within each local area. These details are then published and issued to all professional agencies working in the area.

The LSCB carries executive responsibility for all child protection services in its area, publishes an annual report, and is regularly inspected by the Department of Health. When there is concern about a child, all authorities will follow similar procedures, although there may be some differences in detail.

Referrals and investigations

An investigation of child abuse will often be triggered by a referral that may come from several different sources:
- *The child*: the child may disclose information to an adult.

- *Non-professionals*: the information may come from family or relatives, neighbours and other members of the public; anonymous calls may still have to be investigated, although research suggests the process will stop after the first inquiry.
- *Professionals working with children*: professionals may be health personnel based in the community and in hospital, teachers and childcare practitioners in schools, day-care centres and under-5s groups as well as voluntary agencies such as Childline.

Staff in LSCB member agencies must make a referral to social services if there are signs that a child under 18 or an unborn baby is experiencing or may already have experienced abuse or neglect, or is likely to suffer significant harm in the future.

Referral should usually be within one working day of recognising a risk. Verbal and telephone referrals should be confirmed in writing within 48 hours. Social services should acknowledge referrals within one working day. All referrals should be evaluated within one working day and should establish:

- the nature of the concern;
- how and why it has arisen;
- what the child's needs appear to be;
- whether the concern involves abuse or neglect;
- whether there is a need for urgent action to protect the child or any other children.

If there is no further action, feedback should be provided to the family and referrers. A decision may be made to conduct a fuller assessment of needs, which must be completed within a maximum of seven working days from the date of referral. The possible outcomes are either no further action or instigation of a core assessment.

Core assessments have to be completed within a maximum of 35 working days. Social services departments are responsible for coordination and completion of this assessment, drawing on information provided by partner agencies. Any request for information must be given serious consideration and clear reasons recorded for a refusal. If the assessment is that further support is required, a 'child in need' plan should be agreed with the family and other agencies. This should be monitored and reviewed regularly at a maximum interval of six months.

It is never the role of the childcare practitioner to carry out an assessment but you may be asked to provide information. An allegation of child abuse or neglect may lead to a criminal investigation; do not undermine it by asking a child leading questions or attempting to investigate the allegations of abuse.

The framework for assessing children in need and their families provides a standardised approach to the referral and assessment process.

The assessment will attempt to establish the truth in any allegation, to make a record of the allegations and the evidence, to assess the current risk to the child, to find out if there are continuing grounds for concern and whether protection procedures should be put in place, and possibly offer other services.

The investigation is the responsibility of the child protection team, which may comprise a police officer and a social worker or a paediatrician and social worker. All have received special training and are skilled in child abuse cases. Their first task is to establish contact with the parents of the child plus any other key carers in the

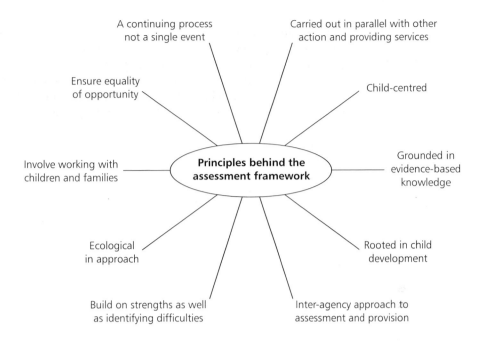

Principles behind the assessment framework:
- A continuing process not a single event
- Carried out in parallel with other action and providing services
- Ensure equality of opportunity
- Child-centred
- Involve working with children and families
- Grounded in evidence-based knowledge
- Ecological in approach
- Rooted in child development
- Build on strengths as well as identifying difficulties
- Inter-agency approach to assessment and provision

Principles behind the assessment framework

child's life. They will then interview the child in the child's home if this is not a threatening place. This may be repeated later at a specialist centre using video equipment, which may be used in evidence in criminal proceedings.

Immediate steps could be taken to protect the child if it was thought the child was at risk. This would nearly always be on a voluntary basis, while further investigation is undertaken, although emergency orders could be sought. There is often less urgency in cases of emotional and sexual abuse than in cases of physical abuse. In emotional and sexual abuse the damage has already been inflicted and a softly-softly approach might yield better results. In physical abuse the risk of injury might be escalating. If it is thought that abuse is taking place within the family, all other siblings would be seen and interviewed. The investigation may require a medical examination to take place. This will usually be carried out in a hospital by a paediatrician. As this may be used in evidence, it will have to be very thorough and may involve an internal examination as well as taking swabs and samples.

The alleged abuser will be interviewed, usually at a police station. This interview will be tape-recorded and may be used in evidence. It is very rare for young children to be interviewed without their parents' knowledge and consent. The investigation would require collecting as much information as possible about the child, the family and the alleged abuser from other professional workers, as all agencies have a general duty to assist the local authority. If the parents are uncoop-

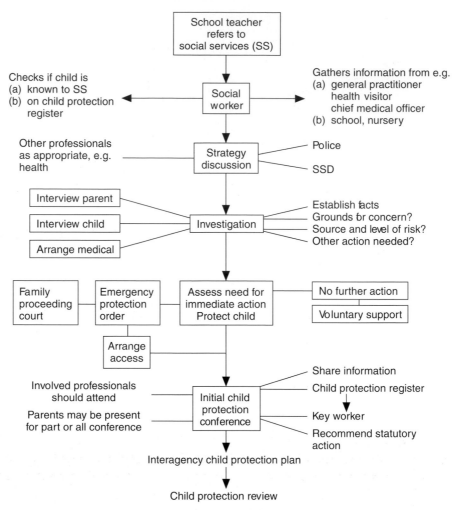

An outline procedure for investigating a case of possible child abuse

erative, a child assessment order may be sought from the court. A Guardian ad litem (page 97) might be appointed to protect the child's interests at this time. A child able to understand the concept of assessment and medical examination may withhold consent.

Following this assessment, if there is no cause for concern, the person with parental responsibility, the child and the referrer are informed in writing. If there are grounds for concern, there will be a formal child protection conference.

Key carers will interview the child at home

Activity

Within the bounds of confidentiality, ask your placement supervisor or line manager if they have attended a child protection conference. Ask what procedures were used and whether the parents were present. What briefing and debriefing did they receive?

Child protection conference

According to *Working Together under the Children Act 1989*, the child protection conference should be held within eight working days with a maximum of 15 days. A conference should also be called if a child from another local authority on their register moves into the area. Social services are responsible for calling the conference. The conference is not called to apportion blame but to:

■ exchange and evaluate information from all agencies;

■ decide on the level of risk and the likelihood of future significant harm;

■ decide if the child needs to be placed on the register;

- decide what action is needed with intended outcomes and timescales;
- allocate a key worker to develop, coordinate and implement the child protection plan;
- identify a multi-agency core group to develop and monitor the child protection plan.

Conferences require several different agencies to be present before decisions can be made. Specialists such as child psychiatrists and experts in family law, who may not know the family previously, may be called to give advice.

As a childcare practitioner, you may be required to attend a child protection conference to present an observation you have made of the child or an assessment of any recent changes in the child's behaviour. You will not be asked for opinions but only for objective evidence, and this is where your observations and record keeping will be most valuable. You may be sent an agenda in advance and the Department of Health has devised a checklist that you should receive before a conference, although it is not always received in time. This will give you basic information about:

- why the conference has been called;
- who will be present;
- the task to be accomplished;
- the decisions to be made;
- definitions of abuse;
- criteria for registration;
- information concerning local procedures.

At the very least, it is useful to know why the conference is being called and what is expected of you at the conference.

Parents and carers will be invited to attend the conference for at least part of the time and will be given the opportunity to express their views themselves or through a representative. The child may also attend the conference if they are considered old enough to understand the proceedings.

If the conference decides that the child is suffering or is likely to suffer significant harm, it will register the child under one or several categories. A review date will be set. Parents should be encouraged to participate in child protection conferences and professionals should inform parents of the information that they are going to present. No additional information should be given at the last minute. The need for registration should be considered separately in respect of each child in the family or household.

Activity
You have attended a conference because a child in your establishment has been sexually abused by a family friend. As part of the child protection plan you have been asked to monitor the child's behaviour and emotional development and to keep detailed records.

Child protection register

The child protection register is held by the social services department and maintained on computer. Children can be placed on the register who are judged to be
'at risk of significant harm' but only after the decision is taken by a fully quorate
case conference where all professional participants have been allowed to express
a view. The decision will reflect the perceived risk of future abuse as well as past
abuse and it is possible to place an unborn baby on the register if someone in the
family is a known abuser. The register provides a central record of children
known to be 'at risk', so that agencies who are concerned about an individual
family can check their current status. Access to the register is usually restricted to
senior officers of any agency, but making this check is an essential part of professional responsibility. Anyone contacting the keeper of the register by telephone
would be called back with the information asked for to ensure that security and
confidentiality is maintained. The register should indicate under what categories
of abuse or neglect the child has been registered, and the position should be regularly reviewed.

The register should contain:
■ full name of the child plus any aliases or 'known by' names;
■ address, sex, date of birth, ethnic and religious group;
■ full names of those who have care of the child, together with information
  about who has parental responsibility;
■ details of the GP;
■ school, nursery, playgroup, etc., attended by the child;
■ date when the child was placed on the register;
■ categories of abuse under which the child is registered;
■ name and address of the key worker;
■ date for review;
■ legal status of the child (any orders which affect the parents' rights, etc.).

Any changes to the information require the data to be amended and all other
agencies to be informed. There should also be procedures to deal with situations
where children go missing, any major incident affecting a child, or when any
child moves to another authority. As part of the continuing action to protect the
child, a core group will be appointed under the leadership of a key worker, generally the social worker. This group will draw up a detailed child protection plan
and may undertake more thorough assessment. The core group will:
■ attempt to establish effective communication;
■ collect information to assist the key worker;

- formulate and implement the child protection plan;
- monitor progress of the plan against objectives;
- set time limits and the timetable for reviews and meetings;
- make recommendations to review conferences about registration and future plans;
- define contact arrangements with the family.

Reviews and deregistration

Reviews should be held at least six-monthly to reassess the child protection plan or to take the decision to deregister the child. At least three agencies should be present for such a decision to be taken. The child may be removed from the register because:
- the risk of abuse has receded within the family;
- the child has been placed away from home and is no longer in contact with the abuser;
- the abusing adult has left the household;
- the child has moved to another area;
- the child has reached 18, has married or has died.

Deregistration does not necessarily mean that social work support is not needed by the family.

CASE STUDY 5.1

Carly, aged 5, has started at your infant school and you are informed by the head teacher that she has recently been removed from the child protection register. Carly's mother never stays to talk to the other parents or to the staff. Carly has not yet made any relationships with children or with adults.

1 What support could you offer Carly?
2 How might you improve your relationship with her mother?
3 What information do you need to know about Carly's background?
4 Would observations be useful, and if so, what method would you use?

KEY TERMS

You need to know what these words and phrases mean:
   care order
   child advocacy centres
   child assessment order
   Children Act 1989
   emergency protection order
   deregistration

disclosure
parental responsibility
partnership with parents
recovery order
residence order
significant harm
statutory responsibility
supervision order

Resources

Archard, D. (2004) *Rights and Childhood*, 2nd edn. Routledge, London.
Donnellan, C. (ed) (1996) *What Are Children's Rights?* Independence, Cambridge.
Lyon, C. (2003) *Child Abuse*, 3rd edn. Family Law, Bristol.
Newell, P. (2000) *Taking Children Seriously*. Gulbenkian Foundation, London.
Stainton, R. W. and Roche, J. (1994) *Children's Welfare and Children's Rights: A Practical Guide to the Law*. Hodder and Stoughton, London.
UNICEF (2009) *The State of the World's Children 2009: Maternal and Newborn Health*. UNICEF.

CLC LEAFLETS

The Child Protection System: A Guide to the Law, 2003.

WEBSITES

www.un.org
www.crae.org.uk
www.ico.gov.uk
www.childrenslegalcentre.com
www.nspcc.org.uk

6 THE ROLES OF THE DIFFERENT AGENCIES IN SAFEGUARDING CHILDREN

This chapter covers:
- The role of the local authority
- The role of social services
- The role of the health service
- The role of the education service
- The role of the legal system
- The role of voluntary groups
- The role of the childcare practitioner
- Male childcare practitioners

If you are working with children who have been abused or thought to be at risk, you will find yourself working as part of a multidisciplinary team that will include representatives from social services, education, the health service and the legal system, and possibly other voluntary groups or organisations such as the NSPCC and the Family Rights Group (FRG). All inquiries into child abuse have shown the importance of all professionals within all agencies working together as a team to protect children, sharing information and coordinating services. Everyone should be clear about their own role and responsibilities, and understand those of colleagues in other agencies.

Each group that you work with will have received different training and may have a different perspective on child protection. A great deal of hard work has to be done to make these disparate groups act together in harmony in the interests of the child. Many misunderstandings between individuals and agencies are due to communication problems and lack of appreciation about roles and responsibilities.

It is important to note that the only agencies with a duty to investigate and the power to protect and, if necessary, remove children, are social services departments, the police and the NSPCC. None of the other agencies have statutory duties or powers to investigate, but they play a role as described in local child protection procedures.

To think about

Children would be better protected if there were a single agency in charge rather than a process of getting disparate groups to work together. Do you agree? What problems might a single agency face?

Role of the local authority

The local authority has a responsibility to ensure the welfare and protection of children, working in partnership with other public agencies, the voluntary sector and service users and carers. In consultation with these agencies the local authority has a duty to plan services for children in need and should take the lead responsibility for the establishment and effective functioning of the Local Safeguarding Children Boards (LSCBs).

Role of social services

Social services departments have specific legal duties in respect of children. They have a general duty to safeguard and promote the welfare of children in their area who are in need and to promote the upbringing of children by their families, providing it is consistent with the child's safety and welfare. They are responsible for providing services appropriate to the child's needs, such as day care, after-school care, respite care, counselling, family centres or practical help in the home. Because of their responsibilities, duties and powers, social services departments act as the main point of contact for children about whom there are concerns.

SOCIAL WORKER

Most social workers, but not all, will hold the Certificate of Qualification in Social Work (CQSW) or the newer Diploma in Social Work (DipSW). These involve courses of study of between two and four years and include college-based academic study and work-based placements. Specific training in child protection is usually given after qualification. The social worker works in office-based teams supervised by a team leader. The majority of social workers involved in child protection are female.

Usually a member of another profession, though sometimes a member of the public, alerts social services to potential abuse, and the case is then allocated to a social worker. The first step is to check records and information held by all concerned agencies: health, education, police, probation and social services. This is to build up as complete a picture as possible of the child and the family, even though it may delay the investigation. The social worker will then interview the person who made the referral, as well as the child, the parents, siblings and any other relevant person. The social worker's difficult task is to protect the child while building a relationship of trust with the family. It may be necessary for the child to be medically examined. In extreme cases the social worker may immediately apply to the court for an Emergency Protection Order (EPO) and find a suitable placement in foster care or residential care. A child protection conference will be convened and the social worker is responsible for reporting on the investigation to all agencies concerned before, during and after the conference.

Consistent with the welfare and protection of children procedures, the social worker must keep the parents fully informed, enabling them to share concerns about their children's welfare, attempting to involve parents in planning and decision making, and showing respect and consideration for their opinions.

The social worker will be continually involved with the family and responsible for the continuing assessment and review of the situation and will be in frequent contact with all members of the multidisciplinary team. The formal end of the investigation may quite often mean the start of long-term work with the family.

The public demands a great deal from social workers, who do not always have the power to implement decisions and who very often have a large case load which makes it difficult for them to follow through each case with the thoroughness that child protection demands.

In his 1999 book *Attachment Theory, Child Maltreatment and Family Support*, David Howe recognises seven steps in the social work process:

1　Identify the problem, concern or need.
2　Gather facts and information by the observation, examination and investigation of behaviour, interactions, relationships and feelings.
3　Classify the facts, information and observations.
4　Assess and analyse the case.
5　Formulate aims including help, intervention goals, the reduction of risks and the promotion of resilience and developmentally protective experiences.
6　Choose methods and sites of intervention, help, treatment and service provision.
7　Evaluate the intervention, help, treatment and service provision.

SOCIAL WORK MANAGER

A social work manager will always be a trained social worker. Some social work managers may hold a management qualification. All will be experienced in child protection work. The conduct of a case is the responsibility of the social work manager, and they will be involved in the supervision and monitoring of the social worker, from the investigation phase through to the long-term plans for the child.

FOSTER CARER

No qualification is required to become a foster carer, but there has been an increase in training in some authorities. A foster carer is assessed, registered and supported by a social worker and gives a home to children who need care away from their own families, either long-term or for a short stay. Some of these children will have been abused. Foster care gives a home to 60% of children growing up in care.

The Children Act 1989 expects the foster carer to be made aware of children's cultural and religious needs and to play a more active role in working with the natural parents of the children in their care. A foster carer's right to act as a parent is limited and they have fewer means of control and sanctions than the parents.

CASE STUDY 6.1

Lee, aged 7, is in foster care. He lived with abusive parents up to the age of 5. The school and his foster parents find his behaviour very disruptive and disobedient. He confronts every decision, he is rude and he upsets other children and adults. He is manipulative and controlling.

1 How might the school and the foster parents work together to present a consistent front?
2 Who might support the foster parents?
3 What might this support be?
4 What method of observations should be undertaken?

Role of the health service

All health professionals in the NHS and the private sector play an important part in ensuring children and families receive the care, support and services they need to promote children's health and development. The responsibility for child protection services across all health service providers lies with the primary care trusts. They appoint a designated nurse and doctor to take the strategic lead in all aspects of the health service contribution to safeguarding children. They are responsible for ensuring that policies and procedures exist and that there are adequate arrangements for consultation, supervision and training.

GENERAL PRACTITIONER

A general practitioner (GP) is a qualified medical doctor who has taken further training. One aspect of this training will be paediatrics, and child protection will be included. This training should be regularly updated. The GP is responsible for the primary health care of the families on their case load. GPs often have excellent knowledge of the families, but they tend not to play a central role in child protection cases and often find it difficult to attend child protection conferences and liaise with other professions. This is unfortunate as the GP is often the first to become aware of indications of child abuse and neglect.

To think about
What reasons might there be for the GP not wishing or being unable to become too heavily involved in child protection cases?

The police surgeon might be the first person to examine the abused child

PAEDIATRICIAN

A paediatrician is a qualified medical doctor who has taken specialist training in child health and further training in child protection. Each health authority is responsible for identifying a senior paediatrician to take a professional lead on all aspects of the health service contribution to safeguarding children. Paediatricians played a key role in bringing child abuse to the attention of the public in the 1960s and 1970s. The paediatrician works in the community to promote health and assess development, and in hospitals to treat sick children; they have a central role in diagnosing physical abuse and also neglect, failure to thrive and sexual abuse.

Historically, paediatricians have been regarded as powerful, and it has been difficult to challenge their diagnoses. The Cleveland inquiry questioned their infallibility. The paediatrician has a key role in the organisation of the LCSBs. The paediatrician can make arrangements for children to be admitted to hospital for assessment, and will be involved in interviewing parents. The paediatrician may be required to give written reports that may be used in legal proceedings and is sometimes required to attend court to present evidence.

HEALTH VISITOR

A health visitor is a trained nurse with a one-year specialist training in health visiting, including issues concerning child protection. Many health visitors are also midwives. Each health authority is responsible for identifying a senior nurse with a health-visiting qualification to take the lead on all aspects of safeguarding children. Working primarily with preschool children and their families, the health visitor visits all families in a specific location or who are attached to a general practice. They will undertake intensive visiting to those children who are at risk of abuse, working closely with a social worker and in partnership with the parents.

CHILD PSYCHIATRIST

A child psychiatrist is a qualified doctor with substantial further psychiatric training. They are not involved in all areas of child protection but may be involved in assessments of individual children and their families. Where appropriate, a child psychiatrist may be asked to contribute to multidisciplinary teamwork and their evidence is highly regarded in cases that come to court.

POLICE SURGEON

A police surgeon is a qualified doctor, frequently a qualified GP, who has a central role in examining children and obtaining forensic evidence for any legal procedures. Some police surgeons are held in high regard because they show considerable sensitivity when they examine the child and because they understand that they might be the first person to help the child come to terms with the abuse.

Role of the education service

After the time spent with their families, children spend most time at school, in contact with a range of people who work there: head teachers, teachers, childcare practitioners, primary school helpers, mealtime assistants and the school nurse. The child might choose to disclose abuse to any one of these people, perhaps someone with whom they feel a special empathy. People who work in a school are in a key position to pick up signs of abuse, and no one more so than childcare practitioners, based on their excellent knowledge of child development and normal behaviour and their observational skills. The role of independent schools in child protection is the same as that of any other school.

Since the Children Act 1989 and the Education Act 2002 the government has published codes of practice to be implemented in all schools:

■ The Local Education Authority (LEA) is required to appoint a designated officer to act as the departmental child protection coordinator. This post relates to children educated at home by their parents, children who are excluded or not being educated at all, and children attending school.

- Schools should be notified by social services of any child who is on the child protection register. This helps them to be alert to the child's pattern of attendance, behaviour and all-round development.
- A teacher must be appointed in every school, the designated teacher, to act as a link with the social services department. This is often, but not necessarily, the head teacher. Every person connected to the school should know the name of the designated teacher. The LEA is required to keep registers of designated teachers and provide them with regular training and support.
- All schools must have a written policy outlining procedures and lines of reporting to social services.
- LEA and LCSB procedures should be followed by all branches of the education service.
- Schools are encouraged to develop curriculum plans that help children develop skills and practices which protect them from abuse, helping them to challenge or speak about distressing situations.

DESIGNATED TEACHER

In his book *Protecting Children*, Ben Whitney suggests that the task of the designated teacher can be summarised as follows:
- *Practice*: designated teachers must make sure that individual cases where children are suffering or at risk are dealt with appropriately by all staff, and that the school meets its legal requirements.
- *Policy*: designated teachers must check that all policies are up to date and workable.
- *Procedures*: clear procedures must be established in schools.
- *Professional development*: the designated teacher is responsible for regular updating of child protection procedures and for arranging training in those procedures.
- *Partnership*: designated teachers should have the opportunity to meet other designated teachers, to share experiences, plan policy and train together.

HEAD TEACHER

The head teacher's approach to child protection may be critical in determining the school's attitude towards the issue, but all educators should be aware that their own behaviour in the classroom should be non-threatening, non-violent and non-judgemental, teaching children to resolve conflict through negotiation and discussion. Young children of both genders are taught caring skills in their play with dolls and in domestic play. Educators should be aware that these skills need to be taught throughout childhood and adolescence, culminating in teaching for parenthood.

SCHOOL NURSE

The school nurse has access to information about schoolchildren and their families and is concerned with health promotion and monitoring development. They have a duty to report suspected abuse, they visit most schools regularly, and they may be permanently attached to a special school.

EDUCATIONAL SOCIAL WORKER

The educational social worker (ESW), also known as the educational welfare officer, is often the link between the school and the community. ESWs should assist the designated teacher in monitoring children whose names appear on the child protection register. They are in a good position to recognise abuse within the family and to act as an adviser to the school.

EDUCATIONAL PSYCHOLOGIST

The educational psychologist is employed by the psychological services department of the LEA. They may be involved in child protection conferences but often their role may be after the abuse has been disclosed, when they help the child in educational and therapeutic contexts.

Role of the legal system

POLICE SERVICE

The police have a dual role. On the one hand, they are required to investigate whether any criminal law has been broken and to prepare evidence for the court. On the other hand, police involvement is used to protect children at risk, always keeping the best interests of the child at the forefront of their actions. They are likely to be involved in investigating serious physical abuse and all cases of sexual abuse. In this area they will be especially trained to work with social workers in interviewing children to gather and assess evidence of abuse.

They are empowered to inform other professionals if an adult has a record of serious crime against children. They are also empowered to help social workers enforce orders under the civil law. The Police and Criminal Evidence Act 1984 gives the police the common law power to enter and search any premises for the purposes of 'saving life or limb'. Under the Children Act 1989, the police have emergency powers to enter premises and offer immediate protection to children who are believed to be suffering from or at risk of significant harm. Exercise of this power could be followed by reception of the child into police protection.

In many areas the police have become very active participants of the LCSBs for the protection of children. After qualifying as police officers, some may choose to train in this specialist area of family violence and abuse; many of them are women. All police services in England and Wales have established child protection units and will take primary responsibility for investigating child abuse cases.

> **To think about**
> Professional people such as doctors, lawyers and priests should be prepared to share information about child abuse with other professionals. Does this break the rules of confidentiality?

PROBATION OFFICER

The probation officer has a statutory duty to supervise offenders effectively in order to reduce offending and protect the public. They are social workers who have completed a specialist option within the course and who is sponsored by the Home Office. Their role is to serve the legal system by advising the court on child and family matters and to represent the best interests of the alleged offender within the legal process.

Like any other professional involved with a family, they are required to be observant and to refer and discuss possible abuse within the multidisciplinary team. If there is concern about the safety of a child who lives in the same household as an offender, they must inform social services. Over the past 30 years, the probation officer has developed a role in working on the treatment of perpetrators of child sexual abuse, often involving community treatment programmes.

Courts

- *Family proceedings courts* are magistrates' courts where all care proceedings from the local authority start. They deal with simple cases such as care and supervision orders, emergency orders, adoption and maintenance and domestic violence.
- *County courts* deal with civil matters only. Some county courts have the authority to deal with cases involving children. Judges and other court staff have specialist training. Complicated cases are moved up from the family proceedings court and heard before a judge.
- *The Family Division of the High Court* deals with complicated cases involving difficult legal issues. It will hear any appeal against a judgement from the family proceedings courts.
- *Courts of Appeal* will hear appeals against decisions of the High Court.
- *The House of Lords* is the court of final appeal.

Proceedings

The child's welfare and future life is the priority of the court. All civil court proceedings concerning child protection are confidential and held in a closed court.

The courts will decide whether or not to grant an order and what is in the best interests of the child. Blame is not apportioned; that is the responsibility of the criminal courts at another time, if appropriate.

The court's welfare checklist should include these items:

- any harm the child has suffered or is at risk of suffering;
- the wishes of the child;
- the child's physical, educational and emotional needs;
- the likely effect of any change in the child's circumstances;
- the capability of the child's parents or carer or other potential carer to provide reasonable parental care;
- any other relevant background information, such as age, sex and culture.

CRIMINAL PROCEEDINGS

Criminal proceedings are entirely separate from care proceedings. The sequence of events in criminal proceedings: police investigation → Crown Prosecution Service → court → found innocent or guilty.

JUDGE

A judge is a qualified barrister who through experience and recommendation has been promoted to the judiciary. They will make legal decisions about the most difficult child protection cases referred from the lower courts. The judge may have had some training in child protection procedures. Judges who sit in the Family Division will have received intensive training in child protection issues. There are some senior women judges with an excellent understanding of the issues. All judges are extremely well trained and qualified to interpret the law.

It is important to understand the different standards of proof in criminal and family cases. In criminal cases guilt has to be proved to the highest standard beyond reasonable doubt, whereas the family courts consider the balance of probabilities. That is why family courts will not simply adopt an acquittal by the criminal court as proof that the accused was not to blame. Judges must make findings on where the blame lies in order to decide whether other children in the family are at risk.

MAGISTRATE

Few magistrates have any formal legal training or qualification. The magistrate is an amateur, reflecting the views and values of the community. They may hold many different qualifications from many areas of work. Some will sit in the family proceedings court to hear public and private cases concerning children. They will process the vast majority of cases that come to court, with only about 15% going to a higher court. The magistrate has to receive some specialist training and have experience in dealing with family matters before they can be nominated to sit.

A judge rules on child protection cases heard in court

COURT CLERK

The clerk functions as the professional legal adviser to the magistrate. They will usually have qualified as a solicitor or barrister. During emergency and care proceedings the clerk plays a critical role in controlling legal activity. As the facilitator and adviser to the magistrate, who is an amateur, the clerk has a great deal of power.

Activity
Visit a court and observe the roles of the people in the legal system.

BARRISTER

If any proceedings concerning child protection reach the county court or the High Court, a barrister will present the court with the case of the local authority, the parents, the child or any other person involved in the proceedings. A barrister is often involved in chairing independent reviews or inquiries into child deaths or failures in the child protection system. Barristers have little specific training in child abuse but may have developed a specialist practice in child protection work.

SOLICITOR

The solicitor represents any of the people involved in proceedings in the lower court, and will instruct the barrister on behalf of clients in the higher courts. The local authority will often use a solicitor from its own legal department. The solicitor will be involved in giving advice from an early stage of the process. The Law Society's Children's Panel is a panel of solicitors whose experience has led to a particular skill in this area. Before being included on this panel, a solicitor is required to undertake some training in child law and child protection issues.

To think about
Is going to prison the most effective course of action for a perpetrator of abuse? What alternatives might there be?

To think about
All professionals working in child protection should receive more training in racial and cultural aspects of child rearing and modes of discipline. Knowing that in some cultures corporal punishment is seen to be the norm, how would you react to a child from such a culture being hit with a strap as a form of discipline?

GUARDIAN AD LITEM

The Guardian ad litem (GAL) is always a qualified social worker, well experienced in child protection work, who will have received additional training before undertaking this role. Employed by the local authority or by a voluntary social work organisation as an independent adviser to the court on the needs and best interests of the child, the GAL can speak on behalf of the child and will help the child come to some understanding of the decisions being taken.

Often involved in the process from an early stage, such as the first or second interim hearing, the GAL will investigate and comment on the original abuse, the child's relationship with the family, rehabilitation and plans for the future. They have a statutory right to access and take copies of records which relate to the child held by the local authority or an authorised person, except for medical records. The GAL does not have any statutory power, but because of their independence and experience, they exercise considerable influence in the child protection process.

OFFICIAL SOLICITOR

The official solicitor will be appointed to cases that begin and end in the High Court, or which are allocated to the High Court from a lower court, often in cases where there are wider, complex issues or matters of public policy. The official solicitor may act as guardian ad litem but will not be a member of any panel of Guardians ad litem. They have excellent access to specialists, such as paediatricians and psychiatrists nationwide.

Activity
Select a recent highly publicised child abuse case and read all the press cuttings. Identify all the agencies and professionals involved.

Role of voluntary groups

There are many voluntary groups concerned in protecting children. The old established ones include Barnardo's, the Children's Society, NCH and family service units. They have a general concern with child welfare and much of their work consists of small local projects in various parts of the country. Broadly speaking, their roles fall within the following areas: helplines for children and adults, provision of direct services, and public education and campaigning.

There are some more recently established organisations that act as advocates, pressure groups or legal advisers to one of the many groups that might be involved in child protection cases. They include the Family Rights Group and the Children's Legal Centre, the National Association of Young People in Care, Voice of the Child in Care, and Childline.

The National Society for the Prevention of Cruelty to Children (NSPCC) has been in existence for well over a century, playing a key role in protecting children. Only the NSPCC among the voluntary organisations is authorised to initiate proceedings under the terms of the Children Act 1989. It has a national network of field social work staff. There has been a recent shift in its role, away from investigative work and towards preventative and therapeutic work. It has developed expertise in training and research and produces some excellent publications. In 1997 it started a major national campaign to alert the general public to child abuse.

Role of the childcare practitioner

All childcare practitioners working in any type of setting need to adopt a professional approach to child protection. Working with young children on a day-to-day basis, childcare practitioners are among those most likely to recognise when abuse is occurring. This can be a very distressing and painful aspect of the work, and you need to be well prepared, psychologically and cognitively, to deal with it sensitively, keeping the best interests of the child in the forefront of your practice. Understand and value the role of all the agencies and the other professional people in this area of work, so that you cooperate and work with them as a team to protect the children in your care.

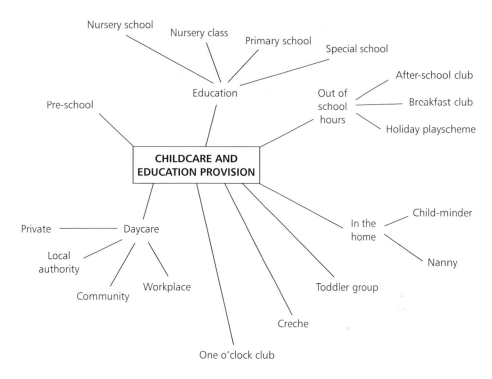

Childcare and education

When working in a multidisciplinary team, adopt a professional approach:

■ Have a clear understanding of your own role and of the function of your establishment; recognise and understand the roles of other professionals involved.

■ Communicate effectively with the team.

■ Take advantage of any joint training schemes or discussion groups, as they will help overcome ignorance and prejudice.

■ Respect differences in values and understand there is a common goal.

One of the many notices that circulate within teams states the following message:

The six most important words in our language: I admit I made a mistake.

The five most important words: You did a good job.

The four most important words: What is your opinion?

The three most important words: Let's work together.

The two most important words: Thank you.

The single most important word: We.

Male childcare practitioners

All childcare training incorporates equality of opportunity into the curriculum, and most colleges welcome male candidates on to their childcare courses for the

Male childcare practitioners challenge the stereotype of an all-female profession

positive male caring role they show to the children, for challenging the stereotype of an all-female profession and, it is hoped, for raising the occupational status of childcare. Research from the Thomas Coram Research Unit has addressed the recruitment of men on to childcare courses. Child protection is an issue often raised when looking at men working with children and this was highlighted by the Hunt Report into the Jason Dabbs case, where a male childcare student in Newcastle was found to have abused over 60 children while on placement. Males working with very young children may fall under suspicion of abuse more easily than female practitioners.

Tutors and trainers should be rigorous about the procedures and policies agreed with placement supervisors and should be alert to the possibilities of students of either gender abusing children. They should be proactive rather than reactive and they should prepare students and placements for the possibilities of abuse of trust. All students in placement must be supervised at all times.

Resources

Butler, I. and Roberts, G. (2003) *Social Work with Children and Families: Getting into Practice*, 2nd edn. Jessica Kingsley, London.

Department of Health (1997) *Making Partnerships Work in Community Care*. Policy Press, University of Bristol.

Murphy, M. (1995) *Working Together in Child Protection*. Arena, Aldershot, Hants.

Pierson, J. and Thomas, M. (2006) *Dictionary of Social Work*, new edn. Harper Collins, London.

Whitney, B. (1996) *Child Protection for Teachers and Schools*. Kogan Page, London.

Whitney, B. (2004) *Protecting Children: A Handbook for Teachers and School Managers*, 2nd edn. Routledge, London.

WEBSITES

www.childrenslegalcentre.com
www.nspcc.org.uk
www.bmj.com

7 SAFEGUARDING CHILDREN

One of the first things you will do when you enter employment is to find out the policies and procedures that dictate the practice of the workplace. This should include procedures to be followed if you suspect a child is in need of protection.

Building relationships

Unless there are obvious physical signs of abuse, you probably would not be aware that a child was in need of protection, unless you knew the children in your care very well and had built up good relationships with them. Children are often reluctant to reveal any unhappiness at home, and young children do not have the experience to compare their home life with that of others. Once you get to know the child and the family and have established a trusting relationship, the child may hint at an unhappy home life. Occasionally your suspicions may be aroused by the parents or carers, who may display a lack of self-control.

In addition to local policy and procedures, you should have access to *What to Do if You're Worried a Child is Being Abused*, 2006, Every Child Matters. This gives clear guidelines and professional advice.

Trusting your intuition is not good enough for a professional childcare worker. Having informed your line manager or designated teacher of your concerns, you should observe the child closely and record changes in behaviour, precocious language or expressions of unmet needs, so that you are armed with some objective evidence. You may then decide to talk to the child's parents or carers, tactfully seeking an explanation for an injury or a change in the behaviour of the child. You may wish to record the parents' or carers' responses. It might be useful to consult your local child protection adviser from the social services department.

Protecting the child in the home setting

WORKING AS A NANNY

If you are working in a family as a nanny and you suspect abuse, it is often difficult to find someone with whom to discuss your suspicions. Belonging to a union or professional association is useful in this case, as it can advise you on how to proceed. If you have recently left college, your tutor may be willing to listen and help you judge the situation. Observe the child or children closely and keep a record of any odd behaviour.

CASE STUDY 7.1

Tina is a residential nanny to George, aged 4 months, and Amelia, who is nearly 3. It is her first job. Both parents work full time. The children's mother, Martha, tells Tina that she expects Amelia to be able to read by her birthday as her cousin already reads, and she is only 2. Amelia is to sit down quietly with Tina for an hour during the morning, while George is asleep, to work at her reading.

Martha does not believe that messy play should be allowed. The children's clothes should always be neat and tidy. Only one toy is allowed out at a time, for a limited period of time. When Martha returns home, she questions Tina about what Amelia has achieved during the day. The children have to be ready for bed and are only allowed to spend half an hour with their mother. Tina never sees Martha show affection to Amelia or George. The only time she expresses any emotion is when Amelia wets the bed, shouting at her. Tina always tries to hide the wet sheets.

1 What can Tina do about this situation?
2 What can she say to the parents?
3 Who might Tina talk to for advice?
4 How can Tina protect both children?

Remember that some families will bring up their children in a way you might feel is bizarre and very different from the way you might have been brought up. They might think that the human body is nothing to be ashamed of, and both adults and children may walk around the house with no clothes on. You might be able to talk about this with the parents if you find it embarrassing. Be careful not to be judgemental or jump to conclusions. Before you enter employment, it is sensible to discuss the parents' attitude to discipline and control. If this is very different from your own views and your understanding of good practice, it might be wise to seek a different post.

If you witness abuse of any sort, you cannot ignore it. Your first duty is to protect the child. If the abuse is emotional or educational, you should try to discuss this with the parents, pointing out the effects on the child and attempting to use your knowledge and skills to show how such abuse would have a later detrimental effect.

If the abuse results in physical injury or sexual exploitation, you should refer to social services or get in touch with the health visitor, the NSPCC or the police. You should not feel disloyal in doing this. You might find it helpful to contact your union or professional association to advise and support you in this matter. You should certainly inform the agency that found you the position.

Be very sure of the facts before taking any action. Taking any matters like this into the public arena may result in you losing your job, and you may even face litigation.

Nannies must be alert to protecting the children in their care

WORKING AS A CHILDMINDER

If you are looking after other people's children as a childminder, you will be registered and inspected by Ofsted. If you have some unsubstantiated concerns about a child, you may wish to discuss it with your health visitor or day-care adviser. If you suspect that one of the children in your charge may be suffering from abuse, you have a responsibility to report it at once to the social services department.

Kirsty childminds Ajit, a 2-year-old whose mother, Abena, constantly appears with cuts and bruises. Kirsty is unable to make a relationship with Abena, who will not enter into a conversation and avoids making eye contact. Kirsty is concerned about Ajit's development, although he has no obvious injuries. Abena arrives late one afternoon with a fractured arm in plaster. She cries and begins to tell Kirsty about her partner's violence.

1 What immediate action should Kirsty take?
2 What action might be appropriate in the long term?
3 How might Kirsty help the child and the family?
4 What sources of help are available?

Activity
What routine records do you have to keep when working as a childminder?

Policies and procedures in an establishment

If you feel concerned about a child, the first thing you should do is look again at the procedures outlining the lines of responsibility. Appendix 5 shows an example of a child protection policy document. The procedures adopted in any institutions should coincide with the procedures outlined by the LCSB. A similar document should also be available within your establishment.

Observations and record keeping

If you notice any physical signs of abuse, such as bruises or burns that are revealed during PE or rest sessions, or when changing a nappy, you must make a written, dated and timed note of the facts immediately; if the facts are not written down within 24 hours, they are not legally admissible. It would be advisable to ask another professional adult to confirm your findings discreetly. It should then be reported at once to your manager or designated teacher, but be careful not to draw unnecessary attention to the child or make the child feel uncomfortable.

All staff need to use similar methods of recording and share the responsibility for this. In some establishments, diagrams of children's bodies may be available to help you record locations and patterns of injuries accurately.

If the child can communicate using language, you may ask the child about the injury. Keep it brief and open-ended; for example, you could say, 'What a nasty burn on your arm! Can you remember how you got it?' Record the child's answer and general response. Do not probe any further or push for an explanation, as this may distress the child.

Where there are no physical signs of abuse and the issue is less clear-cut but you still feel uneasy about how a child has started to behave, it is sensible to keep a diary over a period of time. Note any incidents, accidents or problems that the child has experienced, record any anxieties or fears that the child confides to you, and note carefully any absences, especially if they last a week or more. These records should be dated and completely factual, they should contain no hearsay or opinions, and they should be completed within 24 hours. Page 106 shows an example of a completed record sheet. Inform your line manager that you are keeping these records. Remember that parents are entitled to see these records and observations if they wish. If there has been abuse, you will be asked to produce your written notes at a child protection conference or even in court.

Activity

You are working in a day-care setting and a 4-year-old whispers that his 'uncle' touched him somewhere that he did not like. How would you feel? How would you respond to the child? What might you do?

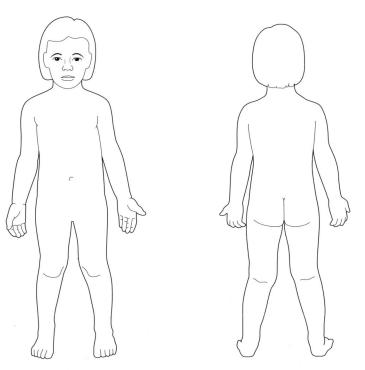

Blank diagram to use when noting injury

ANYWHERE NURSERY

Name   Date of birth   Start date   Class/group

Date Time	Incident	Physical injury	Non attendance	Conversation	Behaviour causing concern	Action	Signature

Example of an empty record sheet

ANYWHERE NURSERY

Name Jane Smith **Date of birth** 10.3.05 **Start date** 8.9.08 **Class/group** Nursery

Date Time	Incident	Physical injury	Non attendance	Conversation	Behaviour causing concern	Action	Signature
30.9.08 10 am		Bruises seen on both arms		Child states she fell off bike		Chart started	CAH
9.10.08 9.30 am 12.15 pm	Child very hungry asked for food at 9.30 am Had 3 helpings at lunch					noted	CAH
15.10.08 –26.10.97			F.T.A	Mother states child unwell Did not see G.P.		Discussed with Line Manager	CAH JF
29.10.08 all day				Avoids contact with adults & peers	Quiet, withdrawn passive	Observations to be made over next week	CAH
16.11.08 3.30 pm	Mother collects child, smells of drink					Discussed with Line Manager	CAH
17.11.08 11 am		?small burns on legs		No response from child	Crying in home corner	Discussed with Line Manager Designated teacher involved	CAH
17.11.08			F.T.A			To contact Social Services	JF

Example of a completed record sheet

Referrals

If you are working in the home setting and have found it difficult to communicate with the parents, you might have to refer a child directly to social services, the family health visitor or the NSPCC. Persevere if the telephone seems to be permanently engaged. In an emergency situation you may have to go directly to the police.

While working in an establishment, it would be unlikely to be your direct responsibility to refer the child, but you must act promptly in informing your line manager, following the procedures set down.

If no action is taken and you feel very sure that the child is in need of protection, you may have to take direct action yourself, even though this might make things very awkward for you. First try to seek the permission of your manager to arrange a consultation with the social services department. If this is denied, you will have to proceed on your own initiative. This will be a rare situation, but you would have to face up to it. Remember that the Children Act 1989 states that 'the welfare of the child is paramount'. You are professionally responsible for your practice and actions. If your manager is not treating your concerns seriously, you might proceed by speaking directly to someone who has specialist knowledge of child protection procedures.

If a child urgently requires medical treatment, an ambulance should be called and the child taken to the local accident and emergency department. Under no circumstances drive the child there in your car. If you suspect that the injury is non-accidental, inform the duty officer at the social services department. Contact the parents or carers immediately, informing them of the specific injury or symptoms, but do not discuss your suspicions of abuse at this time.

Child protection conferences

Once a child has been referred and the matter investigated, a child protection conference may be called. This is where your carefully kept records and observations will be most useful to all the agencies involved. You have a key role at these conferences, as you will have had regular daily contact with the child and the family, and you will have established a warm and trusting relationship that has facilitated communication. Your line manager may accompany you to the conference and this may help your voice to be heard. Your line manager might have a contribution to make in reporting concerns raised by other members of the staff team.

Prepare your contribution in advance and always be factual and objective. You may wish to take your observations, a diary, accounts of conversations and a short written report summarising your concerns. Remember that parents have a right to attend conferences. This might make you feel uncomfortable, but the presence of the parents is in the interest of the child.

If the child is placed on a register and a protection plan is drawn up at the conference, you should be clear about the role you and your establishment will play. You may have some suggestions to make based on your knowledge of the child. Your presence at the case conference will help ensure the discussion remains child-centred, as many of the other agencies will be more familiar with the needs of the parents rather than the child.

The review dates set at the conference may require you to provide written reports on the progress of the child and the family.

A child protection conference, involving relevant agencies, may be called

Abuse in the workplace

If you suspect one of your colleagues of child abuse, you will have to act on your suspicions. The abuse may take one of these forms:

- *Emotional abuse,* such as shouting at children, frightening children with terrifying stories, threatening to punish children, withdrawing affection, isolating a child to sit on a 'naughty chair' or stand in the corner, forcing children to give affection when they do not want to, taunting children in a sarcastic manner, and racial abuse.
- *Neglect,* such as leaving children unsupervised, not providing a stimulating and safe environment, and not changing nappies regularly.
- *Physical abuse,* such as smacking a child, force-feeding, forcing a child to remain on a potty or the lavatory for a long time, shaking or pushing a child, and restraining a child roughly.

- *Sexual abuse*, such as touching children inappropriately, taking a suspiciously long time in the bathroom area when supervising children, making opportunities for time alone with children without a specific, known purpose, and appropriate conversations with children.
- *Factitious illness*, such as pretending one of the children is ill and giving them inappropriate medication or treatment.

To think about
Identify the range of feelings you might have when challenging the practice of a colleague.

If you feel that there is cause for alarm, you should keep a record of all worrying behaviour, noting dates, places and times, children involved, conversations and language, and children's response to such behaviour. These observations should be kept to yourself until you have collected enough data to discuss the situation with your line manager. There are procedures to follow and you may well be involved in contributing to disciplinary procedures.

To think about
What areas of behaviour would you consider serious enough to report a colleague to their line manager? What areas would you feel you might be able to deal with yourself?

In many centres there is a procedure providing an alternative method of reporting concerns using a direct specialist telephone line. Public Concern at Work is an independent organisation that gives free support to individuals who find themselves in a whistle-blowing dilemma. Their lawyers can advise on how to raise a concern about malpractice at work. You can visit Public Concern at Work at www.pcaw.co.uk. Whistle-blowers are never popular, but you have to put the needs of the children before your own. Your union or professional association may be in a position to advise and support you.

Obviously there are degrees of aberrant behaviour and if your colleague behaves in a satisfactory manner in most areas of the work but, for example, insists on standing children in a corner, you could perhaps discuss this, pointing out that it is not good practice to isolate children in this manner. If there is no change in behaviour, you might decide to raise the matter of suitable discipline at a staff meeting.

PROFESSIONAL APPROACH

When working in any childcare setting, be aware that you are in a vulnerable situation. Remarks made by very young children can be misconstrued. The media have made sure that any institutional abuse has been brought to the public's attention, and while this is quite right, it nevertheless makes working in the public domain an area where one's behaviour has to be professional at all times, and open to scrutiny. A research project carried out in 2005 by Piper, Powell and Smith at the Manchester Metropolitan University Institute of Education looked at the growing concern among childcare professionals about touching young children in their care, often resulting in teachers and childcare practitioners holding back from offering children support or comfort. There are steps you can take to prevent being unjustly accused of abuse:

- Make sure your record keeping is up to date. Registers, observations, records of achievement, accident and incident report forms, etc., should all be written up daily and kept in a safe place. If an accident occurs, ensure it is recorded and then witnessed by another member of staff.
- If you are suspicious or concerned about any child or colleague, report these concerns to your line manager and keep a written record.
- Attend staff meetings and local staff support groups.
- Belong to a union or professional association.
- Keep the child's parent or carer and your line manager informed of any incidents, accidents or events that have occurred during the day.
- Ensure that children are well supervised and do not leave them in the care of unauthorised people.
- If a child behaves in a sexually inappropriate manner towards you, record the incident and make sure that another adult knows about it. Some young children like to kiss adults on the mouth. You should discourage this; if it persists, record it and discuss it with a colleague.

PROFESSIONAL BEHAVIOUR IN THE PLACEMENT

1 Do not show favouritism or spend too long with one child unless it is following an observation and with the approval of your supervisor.
2 Do not take children to the lavatory by themselves until you have settled in the placement and are aware of the policy of the nursery.
3 Carry out intimate tasks for children in the presence of other staff.
4 Do not arrange to see children or their families outside the placement on any pretext. Do not agree to any babysitting arrangements.
5 Keep a daily log or diary to record your activities and movements.
6 Use appropriate language in front of all the children.
7 Be circumspect in how you approach children; do not touch or pick up a child who does not want to be touched or picked up.
8 Touches from children that worry you should be reported at once to your supervisor, as well as any other incidents that make you uncomfortable.
9 Do not ask children to keep secrets.
10 Managing children's challenging behaviour should never involve handling a child roughly.
11 Do not shout at children or use a sarcastic approach with children.

As a student you would not perform any intimate task, such as changing a nappy or wiping bottoms without a member of staff there; similarly, it is wise to make sure someone else is present when you first start work at an establishment. With a new child, it may be possible to encourage the mother to stay and carry out these tasks until a good relationship is firmly established. Encourage independence in children and do not carry out any intimate tasks that they are quite capable of doing for themselves.

Make sure someone else is present when you perform any intimate task

Children need affectionate and warm relationships and you should attempt to meet their needs, but if a child tells you that you are doing something that they do not like, stop it at once. Take time to build up relationships. Avoid spending excessive amounts of time alone with any one child.

If a complaint has been made against you, you will probably experience feelings of distress and anxiety, but do not panic. All complaints have to be investigated. This is a legal requirement and everyone involved will be trying to reach an objective decision. Keep a record of all your conversations about the complaint, be they face-to-face or on the telephone. Include times, dates, places and participants. Keep copies of all correspondence. You may wish to seek legal advice, either independently or through your union or professional association. Your setting is required to have a written procedure for when a member of staff is accused of abuse. This is usually included in the child protection policy. A senior member of staff should talk through the procedure with you.

Once the matter has been resolved and you are found to be blameless, you may find it useful to discuss the matter with your line manager or senior manager to prevent such a distressing reoccurrence. You might find it helpful to seek post-traumatic stress counselling. Your managers or your professional association might be able to help you with this.

Recognition of abuse is always followed by specific procedures that have to be adhered to, even though this may result in a stressful and uncomfortable workplace environment. This may be particularly difficult to cope with if you have experienced abuse yourself. Nevertheless, as you fully understand as a professional person, the child has to be protected.

KEY TERMS

You need to know what these words and phrases mean:

child protection conference
child protection plan
designated teacher
line manager
lines of responsibility
observations and record keeping
policies and procedures
referrals
the register
review dates
the welfare of the child is paramount
whistle-blowing

Resources

Department of Health (2000) *Assessing Children in Need and Their Families*. HMSO, London.
Hobart, C., Frankel, J. and Walker, M. (2009) *A Practical Guide to Child Observation and Assessment*, 4th edn. Nelson Thornes, Cheltenham.

LOCAL PROCEDURES

Local child protection procedures are available from local libraries.

WEBSITE

www.teachernet.gov.uk/childprotection
www.everychildmatters.gov.uk/socialcare/safeguarding
www.safeguardingchildren.org.uk

8 WORKING WITH CHILDREN WHO HAVE BEEN ABUSED

> **This chapter covers:**
> - Behavioural characteristics
> - Your role in the prevention of abuse
> - Working with disabilities
> - Supporting children in the criminal court
> - Play therapy
> - Child advocacy centres

The vast majority of children you will encounter as a childcare practitioner will come from stable, happy homes where you will work in partnership with the parents to meet the needs of the children and promote their all-round development. There are some children who are not as fortunate and if you are working with these children, you will play a key role in identifying abuse, observing the children and helping them to recover from the effects of abuse and neglect.

Behavioural characteristics

Chapter 4 describes the short-term effects of abuse on young children. In their 1977 study of 50 abused children, Martin and Beezley describe some characteristic behaviours:

- *Impaired capacity to enjoy life*: abused children often appear sad, preoccupied and listless.
- *Symptoms of stress*: examples are bed-wetting, tantrums, bizarre behaviour and eating problems.
- *Low self-esteem*: children who have been abused often think they must be worthless to deserve such treatment.
- *Learning difficulties*: one example is lack of concentration.
- *Withdrawal*: many abused children withdraw from relationships with other children and become isolated and depressed.
- *Opposition or defiance*: a generally negative, uncooperative attitude.
- *Hypervigilance*: this could be frozen awareness or a watchful expression.
- *Compulsivity*: abused children sometimes feel or think they must carry out certain activities or rituals repeatedly.
- *Pseudo-mature behaviour*: a false appearance of independence or being excessively 'good' all the time or offering indiscriminate affection to any adult who takes an interest.

These behaviour patterns can also be considered as indicators of abuse. Children may react by becoming aggressive or withdrawn.

Abused children may exhibit stress symptoms such as eating problems

Your role in the prevention of abuse

Because of the dire consequences to children who are abused, the whole community — parents, professionals, neighbours and politicians — share the responsibility of prevention and attempting to secure the safety of young children. As a childcare practitioner, your role is to:

- be alert and watchful;
- be knowledgeable – understand the predisposing factors and indicators of abuse;
- teach children to protect themselves by giving them information, awareness and coping skills;
- help parents to understand normal child development and not to have unrealistic expectations of their young children;
- help parents to manage children's challenging behaviour in a positive manner;
- recognise situations when parents may be under stress and offer help when possible;
- be a good role model by presenting a calm, professional manner even when you feel upset or stressed.

Wherever you are working as a childcare practitioner, your planning of activities should include areas where you can encourage children to protect themselves. Teach children to feel good about themselves and know that they are loved and valued. Teach children to trust, recognise and accept their own feelings. Teach children that:

- there is a difference between comfortable and uncomfortable touches;
- safety rules apply to all adults, not just strangers;
- secrets they feel uncomfortable about should be discussed with a trusted adult – any hugs or kisses given by an adult and told to be kept secret should always be disclosed;
- their bodies belong to them and nobody has the right to touch or hurt them;
- they can say no to requests that make them feel uncomfortable, even from a close relative or family friend;
- they can rely on you to believe and protect them if they confide in you;
- they are not to blame if adults hurt them;
- people should not be categorised as good or bad – it is more important to teach children about the danger signs than to watch out for bad people;
- rules of good behaviour can be broken if they feel they are in danger, and it is perfectly all right to fight, kick, bite, punch, shout and scream if they feel threatened;
- they can tell you of any frightening incident – assure them you will listen and believe what they say and will never be angry with them;
- they can help to deal with bullies by being more assertive – if they cannot cope with the bully, they must tell an adult;
- they must not talk to strangers, even when the stranger appears kind and says he or she knows the parents – always tell a supportive adult and never go off with someone they do not know.

There are outside agencies who are willing to come and talk to the children in your care about protecting themselves. The best-known agency is Kidscape, founded in 1984 to enable children to learn about personal safety and teach them strategies to keep themselves safe. There are also books and teaching aids; some are listed at the end of the chapter and some in Appendix 6. The NSPCC, among others, produces a wealth of helpful material such as leaflets, posters and brochures.

Activity
Design an activity for children aged 6–7 to assist in preventing abuse.

Working with abused children

Abuse and neglect have a severe effect on the all-round development of the children involved. An abused child will have strong emotional feelings that will get in the way of learning and discovering the environment. A child who has experienced positive and consistent parenting will have had the opportunity to explore their environment, to make trusting relationships with peers and other adults, and have enough self-confidence to persevere in the pursuit of knowledge, in spite of setbacks. Language will be encouraged and stimulated, and will be a valuable tool in finding out about the world.

Not all children are abused within the family, and a supportive and loving family background helps the child come to terms with what may have happened. A small minority of children who have been abused may be referred to a play therapist. Because play therapists are in short supply, significantly more children will benefit from the skilled attentions of a childcare practitioner. The best way of helping will be to understand and encourage the child to express their feelings, either in speech or in activities that allow emotional expression, and to empower the child to have control over their environment.

Children who have been abused may experience many different emotions, some of them overwhelming. These feelings will depend on their age and on their level of experience.

Provide toys for the child to interact with

Fear:

- of the abuser
- of making trouble
- of losing a significant adult in their lives
- of being taken into care
- of being different from other children.

Isolation:

- because 'something is wrong with me'
- because they feel on their own
- because it is difficult to talk about the experience.

Anger:

- at the perpetrator
- at the other adults who failed to protect them
- at themselves, feeling that they are somehow to blame.

Depression:

- expressed by lack of self-esteem
- expressed by lack of confidence
- expressed by underachievement
- expressed by withdrawal from friends and adults.

Guilt:

- for not stopping the abuse
- for allowing the abuse in the first place
- for disclosing the abuse
- for not disclosing the abuse.

Sadness:

- at losing part of their childhood
- at losing part of themselves
- at losing trust.

Shame:

- at consenting to the abuse.

Confusion:

- because they may still love the abuser
- because their feelings are in constant turmoil
- because they find it difficult to establish new trusting relationships.

Most activities, particularly in the preschool, are designed to give children confidence and a sense of achievement, give them power and control over their environment, and develop their expressive language. Messy play, such as finger painting and clay activities, let children release pent-up emotion in a creative way. Playing with dough is calming, as is water and dry sand play, and lets a child spend time reflectively, without any expectations of producing a piece of work. Conversations can take place with a trusted adult when doing sensory activities, helping the child to express their emotions verbally.

Listening to music and taking part in playing instruments are other outlets for emotion. Making a puppet may encourage a child to say things through the puppet which they might otherwise hold back. Using stories on a one-to-one basis can also be helpful. Domestic play in the home corner, where a child feels private and invisible to adults, creates an enabling environment which may encourage the child to act out their feelings. Provide dolls in the home corner for the child to interact with. For some children, physical activity and outside play may help with suppressed emotions.

It cannot be overemphasised how important it is to continue to monitor the child with observations, record keeping and assessment. Your skills in these areas are highly valued:

- Observe the child at all times.
- Listen attentively to what the child is saying.

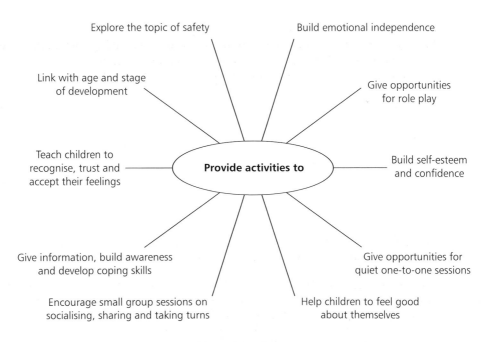

Explore the topic of safety

Build emotional independence

Link with age and stage of development

Give opportunities for role play

Teach children to recognise, trust and accept their feelings

Provide activities to

Build self-esteem and confidence

Give information, build awareness and develop coping skills

Give opportunities for quiet one-to-one sessions

Encourage small group sessions on socialising, sharing and taking turns

Help children to feel good about themselves

Activities for children who have been abused

- Hear what the child does not say.
- Consider and evaluate the child's behaviour.
- Plan positively to help the child, tailoring the daily activities to the current needs of the child.
- Give the child a great deal of attention and encouragement.

GOOD PRACTICE

1   Keep up to date with current practice and procedures.
2   Have a good understanding and knowledge of child development, and understand how this can be affected by abuse and neglect.
3   Display empathy and understanding.
4   Encourage trusting relationships. If the child wishes, respond to the child's need to be held and cuddled.
5   Be professional and do not feel threatened or distressed by the child's expression of emotions.
6   Establish and maintain a professional relationship with the parents or carers.
7   Whenever you can, give extra time to the child on a one-to-one basis.
8   Provide activities every day to allow emotional expression and encourage communication.
9   Have realistic expectations of the child's progress and development. Each small step should be seen as an achievement.
10   Create situations where the child can succeed.
11   Encourage the child to be responsible for others. Taking care of the class or nursery pet helps a child to feel empowered and of value.
12   Accept challenging behaviour. Show disapproval of the action rather than the child.
13   Set limits for the child, as allowing any aberrant behaviour will make a child feel insecure.
14   Value the views and opinions of the child and involve them in decision making and in becoming more assertive.
15   Show the child that you care for them, but resist the temptation to overprotect.
16   Always touch the child gently, and be aware of any movement that the child might see as threatening.
17   Maintain professional standards of observation, evaluation and planning.
18   Maintain liaison with the multidisciplinary team.

Many recent articles about touching children inappropriately have led to a sense of unease among childcare professionals. John Powell, writing in *Nursery World* in 2001, considered what constitutes appropriate touch. Consider whether the touch is:
- welcomed by the child;

- offering a sense of emotional well-being and security;
- reinforcing a sense of positive self-identity and esteem;
- supporting social interaction;
- encouraging confidence and empowerment;
- in response to a health or welfare concern.

He suggests that if the offered touch meets these requirements then it is a practice that may be appropriate, in that it is offering an environment in which young people feel secure and able to develop socially and emotionally.

> **Activity**
> Design and make an appropriate resource, such as a book, a game, a comfort toy or a puppet, to help a child who has been abused.

Disabled children

In 1996 the National Children's Bureau reported that there were 360 000 children under 16 with a disability. Of these, 5 500 lived in residential care, while 16 000 attended residential schools. It is very hard to obtain accurate figures for disabled children who suffer abuse in this country, as very often a disability is not mentioned in the reports of abuse. Studies in America appear to indicate that disabled children are more at risk, as the overall incidence of abuse among disabled children is 1.7 times higher than in the general child population, and these children were found to be twice as likely to experience emotional neglect and physical abuse.

Disabled children, particularly those with speech or learning difficulties, are more vulnerable to abuse. There are several reasons for this:

- They have communication difficulties and are therefore less able to report the abuse.
- Their parents or carers might depend on respite or long-term care and are not always fully aware of what might be happening to their children.
- There may be some problem in recognising indicators of abuse, as they might be attributed to the disability.
- People might be less inclined to believe that a disabled child was abused.
- The behaviour of the child may be very challenging and lead to a lack of control on the part of the parent or carer.
- A child who does not seem to respond to love and affection might deter the parents or carers from persevering in meeting the child's needs.
- Children are more vulnerable if they are in institutional care.
- Children's requirements for intimate care make them vulnerable.

In his 1991 book for Barnardo's, *Linking Child Abuse with Disability*, P. Newport expanded the definition of abuse for disabled children to include:

- lack of stimulation;
- overprotection;
- confinement to a room or cot;

- lack of supervision;
- incorrectly given medication;
- insensitive, intrusive or disrespectful applications of medical photography and medical rehabilitation;
- parents' failure to acknowledge or understand the disability;
- parents' unrealistic expectations.

Other definitions include:

- force-feeding;
- neglect of medical care;
- deprivation of aids;
- physical restraints;
- teasing and bullying within the community.

If you are working with disabled children, either in the mainstream school, the special school, day care or the home, the same good practice is relevant, but it will require more skill and knowledge of the impairment. You will also have to carry out more intimate care for the child, such as:

- toileting;
- bathing, skin care and hair care;
- feeding;
- dressing and undressing.

Until you have established a good and trusting relationship with the child, it is advisable to allow a preferred adult to perform these tasks. This may not always be

Children with disabilities are more vulnerable to abuse

possible, especially if you are working as a nanny. Whatever the situation, make sure you treat the child with respect and sensitivity, working towards the empowerment and independence of the child. Also see the information about Every Child Matters and Every Disabled Child Matters on page 48.

To think about
What disabilities would make a child most vulnerable to abuse? Why?

Supporting children in the criminal court

Although this country has come some way to alleviating the distress of a court appearance by videoing evidence at pre-trial hearings, a child may still have to attend court to give evidence if the defendant pleads not guilty. The stress often leads to the prosecution being abandoned or the case not coming to trial in the first place. *Achieving Best Evidence in Criminal Proceedings*, published by the Home Office in 2001, offers guidance to the police and other agencies during an inquiry about how to ensure adult witnesses and child witnesses give best evidence in proceedings.

Unless you are a social worker or a police officer trained in interviewing children, you will not be involved in the direct interview of the child. You may act as a supporter in an interview, offering mainly emotional support. You cannot act as a supporter if you are a witness in the case. An adult supporter may:

- assume overall responsibility for the welfare of the child witness before, during and immediately after the trial;
- explain the process to the child to suit their age, understanding and mode of communication: this does not mean rehearsing the evidence or discussing its content;
- ensure appropriate facilities are made available to the child before and during the trial;
- liaise with parents or carers, local authorities, police and the Crown Prosecution Service;
- arrange a prior visit to the court, enabling the child to practice speaking in court using a live television link.

As a childcare practitioner, you will make yourself as familiar as possible with the court proceedings so you can answer questions and reassure the child as much as possible.

Play therapy

In the UK, the focus of attention on child protection is often prevention, recognition, investigation and possible legal intervention. Less emphasis is placed on therapeutic strategies to help the child recover. Very few children find themselves referred to a skilled play therapist and, with younger children, a great deal of the work can be done by the childcare practitioner. Several books have been written about the role of the play therapist, and you should consult them if you ever work with children who have been abused.

Ann Cattanach looks at the value of play linked with a number of child development theorists and has some excellent ideas for specialist activities. According to her, 'The play therapy process for the abused child is an exploration through play which helps the child make sense of her experiences in a way which is appropriate to her developmental level. The form and content of the exploration is determined by the child and there are many and varied ways for the child to use play.' She defines three stages in the play therapy process:

- A relationship is established between the child and the therapist so that trust is engendered and the transitional space between the therapist and child is a safe place for exploration. The therapist can become aware of the specific problems presented by the child at this stage.
- The child and therapist explore through toys, objects and dramatic play, in a more focused way, to help integrate and make sense of some of the horror of the past. There is much repetitive play at this stage.
- The child is helped to develop self-esteem and an identity not so bound up in the abusive relationships of the past.

Play specialists have access to a large collection of puppets and dolls, some of which may be anatomically correct. The children may be familiar with anatomically accurate dolls as they may have been used when collecting evidence during an investigation, and videos have sometimes been made of children using the dolls to demonstrate the abuse they have suffered.

Child advocacy centres

In the US, child advocacy centres have been opened, mainly in cities, so that all the agencies who deal with child sexual abuse are under one roof: police, lawyers, social workers, medical examiners and therapists. At a conference in Herefordshire during May 1997, it was stated that two types of therapy were offered: crisis therapy and long-term therapy. The child receiving therapy was thought to remain more 'intact' and more able to deal with the situation. The case of Declan Curren was cited. He was a teenager who hanged himself. He had asked for counselling after being sexually abused; counselling was not immediately available and he had not been able to come to terms with the abuse. Some disadvantages of child advocacy centres are that:

- the child is interviewed in a strange place, not in their own home;
- strangers do the examination, not the child's own GP;
- rural areas are difficult to cover adequately.

The American results showed that:

- probably more abusers were caught;
- the children's lives were made better, as the child's self-image was strengthened immediately;
- information was shared in a speedier and more accurate manner.

As a childcare practitioner, you will have developed a warm, trusting relationship, and the toys and objects you will be working with will be familiar to the child. The room in which you work will be a safe haven and will help the child to relax and enjoy the play that you feel will be most helpful. The great advantage of a play therapist or a child advocacy centre is that long sessions of time working with the child on a one-to-one basis are available, whereas you will have other children to care for and other duties to fulfil.

KEY TERMS

You need to know what these words and phrases mean:

characteristic behaviour
child advocacy centres
children with disabilities
comfortable and uncomfortable touches
emotions
empowerment
independence
observations, record keeping and assessment
play therapy
prevention of abuse
supporting children
therapeutic strategies

Resources

Benedict, H. (1996) *Stand Up for Yourself*. Hodder Headline, London.

Butler, I. and Roberts, G. (2003) *Social Work with Children and Families: Getting into Practice*, 2nd edn. Jessica Kingsley, London.

Cattanach, A. (2008) *Play Therapy with Abused Children*. 2nd edn. Jessica Kingsley, London.

Cattanach, A. (1994) *Play Therapy: Where the Sky Meets the Underworld*. Jessica Kingsley, London.

Cattanach, A. (1997) *Children's Stories in Play Therapy*. Jessica Kingsley, London.

Gorin, S. (2004) *Understanding What Children Say*. National Children's Bureau, London.

Hobart, C., Frankel, J. and Miranda Walker (2009) *A Practical Guide to Activities for Young Children*, 4th edn. Nelson Thornes, Cheltenham.

Macdonald, G. and Roberts, H. (1995) *What Works in the Early Years*. Barnardo's, Ilford, Essex.

Macdonald, G. and Winkley, K. (1999) *What Works in Child Protection*. Barnardo's, Ilford, Essex.

Mullender, A. *et al*. (2002) *Children's Perspectives on Domestic Violence*. Sage, London.

NSPCC (2004) *Children Experiencing Maltreatment: Who Do They Turn To?* NSPCC, London.

NSPCC (2008) *Stress: A Guide for Parents*, NSPCC, London.

Tobin, P. and Levinson-Kesner, S. (2002) *Keeping Kids Safe*. Hunter House, Alameda CA.

Trotter, C. (2004) *Helping Abused Children and Their Families*, Sage, London.

West, J. (1996) *Child Centred Play Therapy*, 2nd edn. Edward Arnold, London.

WEBSITES

www.everychildmatters.gov.uk/_files/86851174DD8BE9FD95B33A66F25B8ZEC.pdf

9 WORKING WITH PARENTS

This chapter covers:
- **Parenting styles**
- **Helping parents to understand abuse**
- **The rights and responsibilities of parents**
- **The childcare practitioner as role model**
- **Worrying behaviour that might cause concern**
- **Working with parents who have abused**

It is part of the professional practice of childcare practitioners to work closely with parents, communicating effectively and regularly, respecting their greater knowledge of the child, and involving them in all decision making. The Children Act 1989 and *Working Together to Safeguard Children* emphasise the need for partnership with parents and, where possible, enhancing and not undermining the parents' role.

Emotional warmth
- Make the child feel valued and secure
- Give a positive sense of racial and cultural identity
- Give warm praise and encouragement
- Give appropriate physical contact and comfort
- Respond to emotional needs with sensitivity

Stimulation
- Encourage intellectual development
- Provide social opportunities
- Encourage communication and language
- Respond to questions
- Promote learning

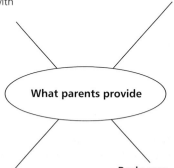

What parents provide

Protection
- Protect from hazards at home and outside
- Protect from contact with unsafe adults and children
- Protect from self-harm

Basic care
- Provide food and drink
- Provide warmth and shelter
- Provide clean and appropriate clothing
- Provide personal hygiene
- Provide medical and dental care

What parents provide

Parenting styles

All families are unique, but sociologists have noted that the way parents interact with their children has been influenced by their culture, class and ethnic group, and the experience of their own childhood. The birth order, temperament and personality of each child will cause parents to handle each child differently. Children from the same family who have the same style of parenting will not necessarily develop in the same way. All families have good and bad times. Children are greatly influenced by the attitudes and parenting styles used by their parents at home.

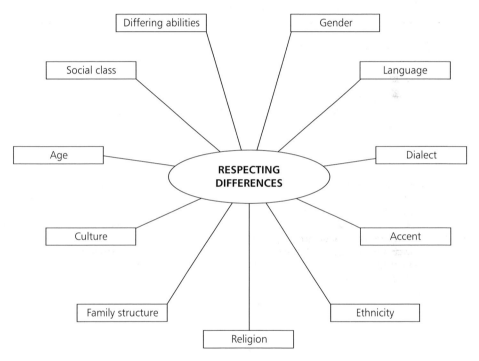

Respecting differences

All parents have their own ideas on how to raise children and it may be very different from the way you were brought up. How parents communicate with, relate to and discipline their children shows their ability and willingness to use their authority as parents. You need to understand the various parenting styles. These styles may change as the children grow or if the family structure changes. Sometimes the mother and the father may not share the same approach, and children quickly learn who to go to for comfort, affection and security. This works as long as the parents respect each other's approach and do not seek to undermine each other.

Parents show by example the skills the children will need later on in life

AUTHORITARIAN

This is the traditional view that parents have absolute control and power over their children's lives. There are hard and fast rules and punishment is swift if they are transgressed. The parents have high expectations of their children, both in aptitude and behaviour. They tend to use physical punishment, fear and threats and are less likely to show physical affection to their children. Children are rarely allowed to question the rules.

When caring for children brought up in this way, you may see:

- fear of learning, in case they make mistakes;
- not admitting to any wrongdoing and lying to cover up a misdemeanour;
- restriction of natural curiosity, not wanting to test the boundaries;
- low self-esteem, and difficulty in making decisions;
- feelings that their achievements will always be inferior;
- poor social and communications skills;
- inability to negotiate and resolve conflict;
- being overly aggressive to others.

There can be a mismatch in the modes of discipline offered at school and at home, with some children unable to adjust to the less rigid regime of the school system, and therefore behaving badly while at school.

PERMISSIVE UNINVOLVED

Parents with a permissive uninvolved style are often coping with many pressures in their lives and find it difficult to respond consistently to the needs of their children. This may be due to demanding jobs or the pressure of coping with day-to-day living. They may not intend to be uninvolved in their children's lives, but the children pick up on how their parents see them as nuisances. They may respond to their children inappropriately and unpredictably, swinging between harsh punishments and extravagant shows of affection. There are few routines or boundaries; the children are left to look after themselves, frequently unsupervised.

When caring for children brought up in this way, you may see:
■ children who appear to be able to care for themselves;
■ extreme risk-taking behaviour, to gain a response;
■ poor self-control;
■ overanxiety to please;
■ lack of self-esteem and a tendency to become depressed.

PERMISSIVE INDULGENT

Many parents with a permissive indulgent style may have been brought up in authoritarian homes. Consequently, they have decided not to place controls on their children, but to bring them up as 'free spirits'. These parents may be very involved with their children, showing them much warmth and affection but placing few controls on them. They try to meet all their children's needs and avoid inflicting their own values and beliefs on their children. Parents will often make elaborate excuses for their child's poor behaviour.

When caring for children brought up in this way, you may see:
■ children who see themselves as the centre of the universe;
■ children who can be arrogant and demanding;
■ poor self-control;
■ lack of understanding and respect for the needs of others;
■ aggression and disobedience;
■ little understanding of limits and consequences.

DEMOCRATIC OR AUTHORITATIVE

Parents using a democratic or authoritative style balance their needs with those of their children. They offer their children warm physical affection alongside clear boundaries and limits for behaviour. They take responsibility for their children, setting rules and making sure they are adhered to. Instead of punishing them, they expect their children to understand when they have broken the rules and to make amends. This family works as a unit, with each member having a share in the decision making, taking age-appropriate responsibility and helping the children to grow into independent, autonomous people:

When caring for children brought up in this way, you may see:
■ children with a good sense of self-esteem;

- an understanding of right and wrong;
- an ability to resist temptation and accept blame;
- an ability to take criticism without resort to aggression;
- self-reliance and self-control;
- ability to make warm relationships with adults and children.

CASE STUDY 9.1

Jenna is 4 and has been attending nursery for one year. Recently she arrived late in the care of her brother, Logan, who is 12. Her behaviour varied between bursts of hyperactivity and tearfulness. When a member of staff asked her where her mother was, she said her mother was at home with the flu. When Logan arrived to collect her, the staff member asked to see his mother and was told that she had broken her leg. The following day they are contacted by social services and told that the mother has gone to Ibiza for a week.

1 Should the staff have released Jenna into the care of Logan the previous day?
2 What information might social services require from them?
3 Should they discuss the matter with the mother on her return?

Activity
- Look at newspapers and magazines to find a wide range of stories depicting parents. How are the parents portrayed? What styles of parenting are the most frequent?
- With a friend, role-play a situation where a 4-year-old is rude to an elderly relative. Using all four parenting styles, show how each parent deals with the behaviour. Afterwards, discuss your feelings and how effective you consider each parenting style.

Helping parents to understand abuse

Most abused children are abused by adults known to them. This could be the father or the mother, a step-parent, a grandparent, an older sibling or any member of the extended family. It could also be someone in whom the parents have placed their trust, such as a neighbour or a babysitter, a sports coach or regrettably even the childcare practitioner. Because this is the case, it is always more difficult for the child to acknowledge that the abuser is someone they know and probably love. If a child is severely neglected, this abuse would obviously be the responsibility of the parents, as they are the ones expected to meet the needs of the child.

Some people might think that children are overprotected today because of the danger of strangers abducting and sexually abusing their children. Statistically, 'stranger abuse' is a minuscule part of abuse; nevertheless, parents should be taught that to keep their children safe they need to:

■ know where their children are at all times;
■ be sensitive to changes in their children's behaviour and look out for any indicators of abuse;
■ listen carefully to their children and discuss any underlying worries;
■ teach their children to say no;
■ teach their children to trust their feelings if they feel uncomfortable with anyone;
■ carefully check out any adult they entrust their child to, such as childminders and babysitters;
■ be alert to any person overattentive to the child or giving inappropriate gifts.

Childcare practitioners will support parents in their relationships with their children by encouraging them to:

■ meet their children's basic needs and ensure their physical care, safety and healthy development;
■ show and express love to their children;
■ communicate regularly and listen sensitively;
■ foster moral, social and spiritual development, helping their children to establish a clear set of values;

Parents should know where their children are at all times

- establish clear and consistent daily routines;
- set boundaries to their children's behaviour and be consistent;
- empathise with their children;
- praise and encourage their children and attempt to ignore challenging behaviour;
- answer their children's questions and encourage their children's curiosity and need to obtain knowledge;
- respect and value their children and apologise when in the wrong;
- have fun and enjoy their children;
- have time for themselves and not exclude their own needs;
- have some understanding of child development and age-appropriate behaviour;
- have regular contact and communication with the staff team.

CASE STUDY 9.2

You are working in a nursery class when Charlie, aged 4, is admitted. He is very shy and clings to his mother, Petula. After 6 weeks Petula is still reluctant to leave Charlie for even a short break to make herself a cup of tea. Charlie has been unable to make any relationships with children or adults and is reluctant to go into the outside play area. You notice that Petula is demonstrating obsessive behaviour, constantly washing her hands and tidying up the book corner and the tables even when the children are still using the equipment.

1 How can you help Charlie develop relationships and become more confident?
2 How can you persuade Petula to leave Charlie in the nursery for a short time?
3 How can you help Petula with her obsessive behaviour?
4 Who can you turn to for advice and support?

It is especially important that you work in partnership with black and ethnic minority families, who often experience discrimination and may well have different child-rearing practices than those you are familiar with. You need to have a sound knowledge of the culture of all the families with whom you are working.

Activity

As a childcare practitioner, how might you support and help parents who do not have English as a first language or who are unable to read?

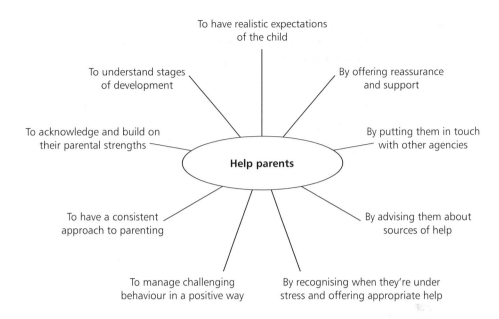

To have realistic expectations of the child

To understand stages of development

By offering reassurance and support

To acknowledge and build on their parental strengths

Help parents

By putting them in touch with other agencies

To have a consistent approach to parenting

By advising them about sources of help

To manage challenging behaviour in a positive way

By recognising when they're under stress and offering appropriate help

How to help parents

CASE STUDY 9.3

Hayley, aged 4, is one of the children in your nursery school. One day her mother, Ellie, looking very distressed, asks to speak to you urgently. The night before, when Ellie was putting Hayley to bed, Hayley started talking about games she was playing in her childminder's house with the sons of the childminder, aged 6 and 8. From what she could gather, these games seemed to involve sexually explicit play.

1 What would your immediate response be to Ellie?
2 Who should you speak to about this?
3 What advice should you give to Ellie?
4 What would be the most useful method for observing Hayley?

P. Mares, A. Henley and C. Baxter suggested in 1985 that if professionals are to work in partnership with black and ethnic minority families to prevent child abuse in our multiracial and multicultural society, they will need to think seriously about the following questions:

■ How far are you seen by the family as a friend and confidant?
■ How far are you seen as representing the law or a form of social control?

- Does the family understand your role and that of other professionals?
- By what value and criteria is the family being assessed and judged?
- Do you carry with you any stereotyped and unhelpful notions?
- Is the system quicker to remove black and ethnic minority children from their families and what is your role in supporting families through this?

Rights and responsibilities of parents

The Children Act 1989 states that parents have key rights and important responsibilities. A new concept of parental responsibility is defined in the Act as 'all the rights, duties, powers, responsibilities and authority which, by law, a parent has in relation to a child and his property'. Parents' rights under the Act include the right to have a say in any decision making about their child and the right to have their views heard in court cases involving their child.

These rights and responsibilities apply to parents, whatever their situation, whether they are married or divorced. Although an unmarried father does not automatically have parental responsibility, he can acquire it if the child's mother agrees or if a court says so. If a court decides a child needs to go into care to be protected, the local authority gains parental responsibility but must share this responsibility with the parents and negotiate how it will be exercised.

The Act emphasises the importance of partnership in looking after children. Partnerships should be formed between social services departments and parents. Social services departments must listen to the views of parents for whom they are providing a service and give them a say in how their child is cared for. Parents with a child in need can best serve their interests by working with social services departments to get the help and support they need. Parents have the right to:

- be informed about actions being taken that concern their child;
- put their case in court;
- be involved in the decision making about their child when their child is being looked after by the local authority;
- have the court resolve disputes over contact with the child;
- be told of any applications to court, unless the situation is so serious that the local authority must act immediately.

The Children Act 1989 has spelled out for parents their rights and responsibilities, and you will need to be conversant with the Act when working with parents.

To think about
Do you agree that all parents should have these rights? Do you think there are other rights they are entitled to?

CONTACT ARRANGEMENTS

More than 46 000 contact orders are issued by the UK courts every year. Less than 3% of applications for paternal contact are refused. The NSPCC believes a legislative oversight is risking the lives of many children, as abusive parents continue to be allowed unsupervised contact with their children following separations. Since 1998 at least 15 children in England and Wales have been killed by separated parents or step-parents as a result of contact arrangements. The NSPCC believes most of these deaths could have been prevented if improved legislation had been in place.

A 2003 joint NSPCC and Women's Aid report, based on a survey from 178 domestic violent refuges in England and Wales; illustrates the inadequacy of the current laws. *Failure to Protect? Domestic Violence and the Experiences of Abused Women and Children in the Family Courts* found that:

- 18 children were ordered to have contact with parents who had committed offences against children and 64 children were ordered to have contact with parents whose behaviour previously caused children to be placed on the child protection register; 21 of these children were ordered to have unsupervised contact with the abusive parent.
- 101 children were ordered to live with an abusive parent.
- 27 respondents say they know of local cases where a contact visit with a violent parent has resulted in a child being significantly harmed. These cases involved abductions, physical or sexual abuse, emotional abuse and trauma.
- 46% of respondents know of cases where a violent parent has been able to use contact proceedings to track down their former partner.

To tighten this loophole, the NSPCC wants specific laws introduced that ensure parents, step-parents or carers are only given unsupervised access to children following separation, where the courts can be sure that no physical, sexual or emotional abuse will take place and that the child will be safe.

In March 2005 a committee of MPs concluded that separated and divorced fathers get a raw deal from the family justice system in England and Wales. This is mainly due to inbuilt delays in the system and tactics used by some mothers to try to deny contact. Judges also had limited power to ensure their contact orders were obeyed. It was suggested that parents should be given help to resolve their disputes by negotiation with the courts as a last resort.

The Children's and Family Court Advisory and Support Service (Cafcass) is to be given a new role helping to facilitate contact arrangements for families. The committee rejected calls by some fathers' groups for 50:50 parenting time. There are now contact centres often managed by volunteers, where children can be in contact with the estranged parent under supervision.

Childcare practitioner as role model

As a childcare practitioner, you are a carer and an educator. These are the same roles that parents fulfil, and children and parents can learn from your example how to care and form relationships with other people. As a professional person, you will naturally show respect and a positive regard for the welfare of the children in your care at all times.

There are certain situations that parents find stressful. The NSPCC has named seven stressful behaviour situations:

- the child who will not stop crying;
- defiance and disobedience;
- children squabbling;
- temper tantrums;
- unfavourable comparisons with other parents by the child;
- refusing to go to bed;
- moodiness and argumentativeness.

To think about

How many more stressful situations can you think of? What strategies might you teach parents to understand and cope with this behaviour?

By the way you react to such situations with patience and empathy, you are teaching a very valuable lesson to the young people in your care. Many of the skills you display are the skills that children will need when they are parents. Your appropriate response to challenging behaviour will have an impact on the child and will be seen to be fair by all the children in the group. Your meticulous attention to equal opportunities will ensure that all children reach their potential and are not trapped in stereotypical roles. The way you listen carefully to children and parents will show how much you respect and value their views and opinions. You will be able to advise families if they are going through stressful times, pointing out helplines such as Parentline and finding local information for parents and carers. Most boroughs have leaflets especially written for parents, often in many different languages.

You will reject violent responses to situations and show children how to respond in an assertive fashion rather than resorting to aggression. Observing and assessing children's individual needs will show you which children might need some individual attention from time to time, while you always have time for all the children in your care. You will at all times display a commitment to equal opportunities and antidiscriminatory practices. It is natural to enjoy the company of some children than to others, but you will not allow yourself to show any favouritism.

By attempting to adopt this pattern of behaviour at all times, you will be showing by your example the skills the children will need later on in life when they become parents themselves.

Offer support and encouragement to parents

Worrying behaviour that might cause concern

All families behave differently, and some of the following factors might occur from time to time in families where there is no question of abuse. Several of these signs exhibited over a period of time should cause concern:

- frequent smacking and shouting at babies and children, often for behaviour that is developmentally normal, such as a toddler wetting their pants;
- expecting the child to be the parent, giving love and comfort to the adult;
- parental indifference to the whereabouts and safety of their children;
- barking orders at a child, without displaying patience or clear explanations of what is expected;
- never giving praise or encouragement;
- unreal expectations of appropriate behaviour;
- discouraging the child's natural curiosity and not providing enough stimulation;
- seeing the normal behaviour and actions of a child as a deliberate act to upset and annoy the parents;
- frequent rows and disagreements between the parents and other family members, perhaps leading to violence.

CASE STUDY 9.4

You are working in Year 2 in the infant school. Letitia, aged 7, comes to school dirty, frequently smelling of urine and sometimes with bruises on her arms and legs. You are told that her mother has mental health problems and is often in hospital. There are three other children in the family, one of whom is a new baby, and Letitia tells you she is expected to look after the 4-year-old and the toddler, get them dressed and take them to the park at weekends.

1 How could you help Letitia in the short term?
2 Do you need more information about this family?
3 What agencies might be involved in helping the family?
4 What action should the infant school take to keep the children safe?

Working with parents who have abused

One of the most useful things you can do is to show parents how to cope with the needs of children and their sometimes challenging behaviour. All children are lively, and challenging adults is part of their development. It is unrealistic to expect small children to be quiet and well behaved day in, day out. Physical abuse is occasionally caused by stressed parents or carers not being able to cope with what is really quite normal behaviour, particularly if they are depressed and isolated. If working as a nanny, you may well have experienced some of these feelings yourself, but as a trained professional you will have the resources to cope with them. Encourage the parents to respond by:

■ taking a deep breath and counting to ten;
■ remembering they are mature and do not need to react like a child;
■ understanding and redirecting their anger, perhaps by punching a pillow;
■ remembering that young children can often be diverted by offering another activity;
■ going into another room for a short time, away from the child, collecting their thoughts and giving themselves time and space to evaluate the situation;
■ contacting someone on the telephone to express their feelings;
■ using local resources such as drop-in centres and parent centres;
■ going outside to scream, shout and let out their feelings, beyond the child's sight and hearing;
■ trying to keep a sense of proportion.

If the person suspected of committing abuse is one of the child's parents, the other people in the family will need your support and advice as they will be confused and upset about what has happened. They may need someone to listen to them in a non-judgemental way, or they may need information and help. They will be very important to the child's eventual recovery, and you will need to be as sensitive and supportive to them as possible.

You may be working with children where abuse and neglect have been diagnosed while they are attending your establishment, or social services may request a placement for a child as part of a child protection plan. In some areas of the country there may be family centres where you may be working with the family along with other members of a multidisciplinary team, such as psychotherapists and social workers.

Whatever the type of abuse, if you find yourself in the position of working with parents who have abused, you will attempt to:
- acknowledge your feelings and seek opportunities to express them appropriately with colleagues and line managers;
- always remember that you need to work with the parents for the good of the child, so you need to establish a working relationship;
- avoid colluding with the parents through fear of aggression;
- deal with the isolation the situation might demand;
- talk and liaise with the other agencies concerned with the case;
- be aware of the child protection plan for this family;
- record conversations and decisions taken with the family, using plain jargon-free language;
- request supervision of your work by a competent line manager;
- acknowledge and relieve the stress of the whole family.

Remind yourself that when you are working with parents you are helping the child and playing a part in breaking the cycle of abuse. Try to assume a non-judgemental attitude and refrain from questioning the parents about the abuse or from challenging information they may give you; this is the task of other agencies. If the parents are coming to your establishment as part of a child protection plan, take time to introduce them to the unit and the routines, giving them as much information as possible about the care of the child.

CASE STUDY 9.5

The social worker asked the school if they would admit Andrew into the nursery class, even though his chronological age was 6. Andrew had a much loved older brother, who was developmentally normal. Andrew had been rejected at birth, and his mother refused to feed him.

When he came on the first day, he did not look at all out of place. He was short and thin and you would think he was no more than 3 years old, especially when you tried to have a conversation with him. His speech was delayed and his comprehension immature. His muscle tone was poor and he often fell down for no apparent reason. He spent a lot of the day alone in the book corner, rocking to and fro.

The nursery team gave him three meals a day in the nursery: breakfast, dinner and a cooked tea. This did not help Andrew over the weekends or during the school holidays. Then the mother was asked to attend the mealtimes; although very reluctant at first, she was eventually persuaded to help prepare the meals and to sit with Andrew while he ate. This seemed to break the cycle of neglect and she came to accept Andrew as part of the family.

1 Why might some mothers neglect their children?
2 In settling Andrew into the nursery, how would you try to involve Mosi's mother in the process?
3 What particular observations might be helpful?
4 How might you prepare Andrew and his mother for entry into the infant school?

Listen to what they are saying and express appropriate concern and kindness while remaining objective and empathetic. You will need to foster the parents' self-respect and improve their self-image. It is hard for parents to understand where they have gone wrong and they have to cope with the close scrutiny of their parenting practice by many different people, often finding it difficult to have a clear idea of what they are meant to achieve. Although the task is challenging for the childcare practitioner, you will not be working in isolation and it is very worthwhile.

GOOD PRACTICE

To encourage good parenting skills:
1　Present yourself as a good role model in all areas of childcare. Use a non-threatening approach at all times.
2　Build a trusting relationship with the parents, working with their strengths rather than their weaknesses.
3　Use praise and encouragement as positive reinforcement when the parent shows appropriate behaviour.
4　Work with the parents in planning the child's future care and development.
5　Listen to the parents and try to establish what particular areas of care they find most trying.
6　Explain to the parents which behaviour of the child is quite normal for the stage of development.
7　Give help and information in dealing with any behaviour the parent finds difficult.
8　Discuss the importance of a consistent response and suggest appropriate and alternative ways of socialising the child.
9　Promote equality of opportunity.

KEY TERMS

You need to know what these words and phrases mean:
    challenging behaviour
    discrimination
    equal opportunities
    parental responsibility
    parenting skills
    partnership with parents
    role model
    stranger abuse
    stresses of parenthood
    worrying behaviour

Resources

HMSO (1995) *The Challenge of Partnership in Child Protection: Practice Guide.* HMSO, London.

Hobart, C., Frankel, J. and Miranda Walker (2009) *A Practical Guide to Working with Parents*, 2nd edn. Nelson Thornes, Cheltenham.

NSPCC (2008) *Stress: A Guide for Parents.* NSPCC, London.

Peake, A. and Fletcher, M. (1997) *Strong Mothers*. Russell House, Lyme Regis, Dorset.

Platt, D. and Shemmings, D. (1996) *Making Enquiries into Alleged Child Abuse and Neglect: Partnership with Families*, new edn. NSPCC, London.

Waldfogel, J. (2001) *The Future of Child Protection*. Harvard University Press, Cambridge MA.

WEBSITES

www.everychildmatters.gov.uk/_files/86851174DD8BE9FD95B33A66F25B82EC.pdf

www.parentingtoolbox.com

10 COMMUNICATION

> ## This chapter covers:
> - Listening to children
> - Disclosure of abuse
> - Record keeping
> - Communicating with colleagues
> - Confidentiality
> - Expressing yourself at child protection conferences
> - Giving evidence in court
> - Feelings
> - Dealing with stress

Good and useful communication is needed in every aspect of a childcare practitioner's work, and nowhere more so than in child protection. You have to listen very carefully to young children who may wish desperately to tell you something but have not yet developed enough language to do it coherently. Be careful in the way you speak to children whom you fear may have been abused, and be tactful and non-judgemental in your dealings with their parents. You must be ready to listen and to talk to colleagues, always remembering the issue of confidentiality. You will need to be confident enough to express yourself clearly at child protection conferences, among strangers, and be ready to give evidence in court in the unlikely event that you are called as a witness. You need to be able to deal with your own feelings and to cope with the subsequent stress and distress.

Listening to children

It is comparatively recently that children have been listened to seriously when they attempt to reveal aspects of their home life that may give cause for concern. It was considered prudish to be shocked at overt sexual language or behaviour from very young children, as this was thought to be a stage in their normal development and, like swearing, it would go away if it was ignored. Nowadays it is realised that children's remarks have to be listened to carefully, in the same way that some drawings might arouse suspicion. However, you must remember that not every remark or painting is cause for concern, as some households are much more open than others in how they speak and behave in front of their children.

Nevertheless, even if you think there is little likelihood of abuse, you must listen carefully, as the main purpose of effective listening is to enable the child to explore their feelings in more depth. Social listening is often partial and superficial, and it is difficult in a busy setting to pay attention to just one child and not be distracted by everything else that is going on around you. You need to get the balance just right by remembering the rights of the child, the rights of the family and the requirements of the legal system. There may be a conflict between your professional responsibilities and your personal feelings. Your professional responsibilities have to be met, even if you later have to seek help and support to allow you to cope with your fears and feelings about the issue. To be a good listener you need to:

- Build a good warm relationship with the child.
- Avoid doing most of the talking.
- Give the child time to talk to you.
- Find a quiet place without competing demands on your attention.
- Try to create empathy by showing respect and understanding.
- Do not complete a child's sentences.
- Listen to the words and the tone of the child's voice.
- Use your knowledge and experience to understand what the child is saying.
- Watch the child's body language.
- Be aware of your own body language and the messages you may be communicating.
- Be aware of your own reactions and responses to the conversation.
- Be careful not to jump to conclusions. Keep an open mind and do not ask any leading questions.

Listen to the child but do not press for information

Disclosure of abuse

In his report of the inquiry into the death of Victoria Climbié, Lord Laming stressed that nobody listened to Victoria. Where allegations have been made, his report recommends that the child must be seen and spoken to within 24 hours, no case should be closed until the child has been seen alone, and an interpreter should be provided for children whose first language is not English.

In 1998 the NSPCC published a review of research on child protection, identifying common mistakes in initial assessment and inquiries. The mistakes are set out in *Working Together to Safeguard Children* and one mistake is that 'not enough attention is paid to what children say, how they look, and how they behave'.

If you now find yourself in the position where a child is disclosing abuse to you, you need to respond in a way that will not further harm the child. Be very patient with silences, allowing the child to regroup their thoughts. As a way of prompting, reflect back the last thing the child has said; for example, if the child says, 'He was staring at me,' you could reply, 'Staring at you?' Never ask leading questions such as 'Where did he touch you?' This may lead the child into making a response that may not be true. A young child will usually try to please an adult and may guess which answer is wanted. Open questions that require a broad response, such as 'How did you feel about that?' or 'Tell me about it!', are better than closed questions, which require only a yes or no response. Always:

- attempt to make the child feel secure and safe in disclosing to you;
- reassure the child stating that you are pleased to have been told, that you believe them and that they are not to blame for the abuse.

Never:

- look shocked or disbelieving;
- express criticism of the perpetrator;
- promise to take an action that you may not be able to carry out.

When coping with disclosure:

1 Keep calm. Do not panic or overreact. Remember that you are not angry with the child but at what happened. Children can mistakenly interpret anger or disgust as directed towards them.
2 State that you believe the child. Young children rarely lie about abuse.
3 Give positive messages such as 'I know it's not your fault' or 'I'm pleased that you told me'.
4 Ensure the child understands they are not to blame.
5 Listen to the child's questions and answer them honestly but do not press for information.
6 Do not question the child, as other agencies will have to interview the child and information may become distorted.
7 Reassure the child that you will protect and support them.
8 Respect the child's privacy and rules of confidentiality but never promise to keep secrets you are duty bound to report. Let the child know that you are having to talk to someone else.
9 Follow the procedures set down in your workplace for reporting and investigating the abuse.
10 Use language appropriate to the child's level of understanding; do not put ideas into the child's head.
11 Make an immediate timed, dated and signed record of the conversation.
12 Tell the designated person for child protection as soon as possible on the same day.

Develop your listening skills

13 Make sure the child is clear about who is taking what action and when.

14 If you work from home, ring social services or, if unsure, ring the NSPCC helpline.

You need to be aware that some children:

- may have been threatened by the perpetrator;
- may have been told not to tell anyone as they or the perpetrator might be taken away;
- may feel the need to protect other members of the family;
- may be feeling guilty because they have been told by the perpetrator that they are to blame;
- may also not trust adults and believe that it is not safe to tell;
- may think they will not be believed anyway;
- may have tried to tell before and not been listened to.

Record keeping

If possible, find a quiet place and endeavour to write an accurate record of the conversation; be scrupulous in leaving out your own feelings and staying objective. Make a note of the date, time and the place where the conversation was held. Make a note of any dates and times mentioned and the key phrases used by the child. If the child uses euphemisms such as 'willy', write down those euphemisms rather than interpreting the words yourself. These notes and records must be made and signed by you within 24 hours if they are to be legally admissible. When giving this record to your line manager, make a copy for yourself and keep it in a safe and secure place. The procedures of the establishment will now be followed. Try to do some careful observations of the child's behaviour and record any conversations which might take place during the time of the investigation.

All establishments should make sure their documentation is continually updated. The record should show the current and previous names of the child, the address, date of birth, GP, day-care, nursery school history, the names of all adults who have parental responsibility, and who to contact in an emergency.

All records are legal documents and can be used as evidence in court proceedings as well as being read by the parent. Parents may also have access to copies of correspondence that are held by a third party such as social services. Sharing of information should be in accordance with the Data Protection Act 1998 (see Chapter 5).

Communicating with colleagues

COMMUNICATING WITH THE TEAM IN THE WORK SETTING

Confidentiality constraints mean that any concerns you have about a particular child can be discussed only with people who need to know. For example, you will have informed your line manager as soon as the child has disclosed to you. If you are working in a school, the head teacher and the designated teacher will also be in consultation. In a nursery or preschool you will inform the person with overall responsibility; the same goes for a day-care centre.

> **To think about**
> Policies on how to deal with disclosure may vary in different establishments. Discuss these differences with your group.

Hold conversations privately and store documents safely under lock and key. Do not gossip about the child or the family. Keep all lines of communication open as the case is referred to the social services and the procedures are put into operation. Ideally this communication will allow you to be fully informed of events and developments as they take place, so you can do your best when planning work with the child and the family.

COMMUNICATING WITH OTHER AGENCIES

Since the inquiry into the death of Maria Colwell, communications failures between child protection agencies have been seen as a contributory factor in some cases of serious injury or even death. Subsequent inquiries have reinforced the critical importance of good multidisciplinary communication in preventing and recognising abuse and neglect.

Research has indicated that good multidisciplinary communication is facilitated by:

- all professionals feeling valued for their contribution;
- good interpersonal skills involving active listening and clear articulated speech without the use of jargon;
- valuing and respecting the work of others;
- participating in good interdisciplinary training;
- understanding each other's roles;
- recognising and challenging stereotyping and racism;
- dealing calmly with conflict;
- never attempting to take over another agency's work.

The Children Act 1989 has caused a greater emphasis to be placed on good communication with parents.

Confidentiality

The degree of confidentiality should always be governed by the need to protect the child. In child protection practice, disclosure of confidential information can be justified:

- with the consent of the parent or carer and/or the child;

- without consent when the disclosure is required by law or by court order;
- without consent when it is considered necessary in the public interest.

There may be conflict among some professionals when a child discloses and asks them not to take the information further. This issue has been addressed by ChildLine, which offers children complete confidentiality unless they are in a life-threatening situation. Very serious incidences of sexual abuse have occasionally led to the police being informed. Children know that they are in control of the situation and that it is up to them whether they wish the matter taken any further. As a childcare practitioner, you are unlikely to have children in your care who are old enough to request confidentiality. Your primary responsibility is to act in the child's best interest and to share relevant information on a need-to-know basis with other professionals who have a duty of care towards the child.

Expressing yourself at child protection conferences

If you are invited to attend a conference because you have information and observations concerning a child, you will probably find yourself quite anxious. Your line manager or designated teacher may be invited to attend with you, and you will have the opportunity to discuss your contribution beforehand. The best way to ease your worries is to be well prepared and organised. You will receive general information and an agenda before the meeting. Familiarise yourself with everybody's role and make sure you understand the procedures. Remember:

- Accept that you will be nervous beforehand and brush up on the relaxation techniques that work for you.
- Be positive and confident in your role.
- Monitor your vocal expression, thinking about volume, pitch and speed, and take your time.
- Articulate your words more clearly than usual, as you are speaking to a larger group.
- Prepare any written statements, observations or general notes before the conference so that you can use them in response to questions.
- Make copies of anything you may wish to distribute prior to the conference, confirming with your line manager that you are not breaching confidentiality.
- If you should suddenly go blank, pause, take a breath, refer to your notes and carry on; this happens to most people at some time.
- Most people present will feel anxious and this may be expressed in different ways; an experienced chairperson will understand this and attempt to keep the meeting focused.
- The parents may be present.
- Some explicit terms may be used that you might find embarrassing to express or to hear; prepare yourself for this. When you are reporting the speech of the child, repeat the exact words they said to you.

- Concentrate on the task; you are there to communicate an important message from the child.

Working Together to Safeguard Children states that all professionals attending a conference should prepare a written report. All reports should distinguish between fact and observation, allegation and opinion. Professional opinion should be supported with relevant evidence. All information should be clear, concise and relevant to the protection of the child. Throughout your course, taking part in group discussions and contributing to seminars and debates will prepare you well for this type of activity during employment.

In your written report be careful to distinguish between fact and observation, allegation and opinion

Activity

In your group, take it in turns to read out a general observation you have made during your present placement. You do not have to choose an observation on a child that is causing you concern. Expect questions by the group and try to prepare your answers in advance. This will enable you to practice standing in front of a group and being questioned on your report.

Giving evidence in court

In the unlikely event that you are asked to go to court as a witness, you should be well prepared. Find out about the court procedures in advance. There may be a delay between the incident and the court hearing. Make your notes and records as full as possible. In court you are allowed to use informal notes you have made for your own benefit.

Court proceedings often involve a great deal of waiting around. You may be given a specific time to attend rather than being expected to be there for the whole of the proceedings, but there may be delays or the proceedings may be cut short. Occasionally, the hearing may be rearranged or rescheduled. Take something to occupy yourself, such as a book or a journal.

If you have to appear in court, this will probably be at the instigation of the local authority and you will have to make a statement to their solicitor. You may have to describe events that you have witnessed or your observations of the child's behaviour. The solicitor should advise you, and your line manager should be available to support you through the process. This is particularly important after the appearance, when you will want to discuss and reflect on the experience.

Care proceedings concerning child protection cases are informal and not open to the general public. All those involved sit at the same level. No one is on trial. Everyone has the same goal: to identify the best interests of the child.

GOOD PRACTICE

When attending court:
1   Acquire as much information as you can before the event.
2   Keep your records meticulous and up to date.
3   Remember to take all your records and notes with you.
4   Look neat and tidy, and be punctual.
5   Listen carefully to any questions.
6   Reflect for a moment before you respond to questions.
7   Speak as clearly as possible.
8   Be objective; stick to the facts, unless an opinion is sought.
9   Be truthful; do not elaborate or waffle.
10 If you do not understand a question, ask for it to be repeated.
11 If a question is repeated and you still do not understand, say so.
12 Concentrate on the question in hand; try not to anticipate the next question.

Feelings

Whenever you read in the media about a small child being abused or neglected, it will probably arouse your feelings. Now imagine your feelings if the abuse should happen to a child in your care. Initially, you will be shocked and horrified, and may view the evidence of abuse with some disbelief. As you begin to accept the situation, you may experience waves of anger, revulsion and disgust towards the perpetrator. Then the professional side of you will take over and you will realise that your job is to help the child and the family come to terms with what has happened, and that objective observations and reports will be valuable at child protection conferences and, if necessary, in court.

You will probably feel apprehensive and nervous if you are asked to give evidence, particularly if the child first disclosed the abuse to you or if you are the person who picked up the evidence of abuse. When first working in a multidisciplinary setting, you may feel some reluctance to contribute to arguments produced by highly qualified and knowledgeable professionals. But remember that you are the professional in daily contact with the child and your role is to ensure their voice is heard.

At first, the people to whom you reported the abuse might not have been convinced, and you may have experienced feelings of frustration at not being able to put the case across sufficiently well to ensure the child was protected. It has been estimated that 10% of the population have suffered some form of abuse or neglect, and if you are one of these people, the discovery of abuse might reinvoke the feelings you had in the past, perhaps making it more difficult for you to accept that abuse is occurring and to take action. But as a professional, you know you have to put your own feelings to one side and act in the interests of the child.

Discovery may arouse strong feelings of guilt, firstly because you had not recognised the abuse earlier, and secondly because you were slow to accept what was happening. You might feel that you could have prevented the abuse in some way. This would not be true, and none of it is your fault. You are not the perpetrator. If the perpetrator is someone you know and have built a relationship with, it often destroys your faith in humanity for a short while. If the perpetrator is one of the parents, you have to get over your feelings of anger and betrayal and your reluctance to communicate with them. You will need to remain on professional terms, so as to help the child.

Remember that most parents do love their children and want the best for them. Focus on the needs of parents rather than the injuries of the child. You should not be surprised by repeated rejection from the parents, who lack self-esteem and trust, and who are experiencing fear, guilt and remorse. Be careful not to overidentify with the parents so that your objectivity becomes affected. Some staff may find it difficult to remain working in an establishment following a court case and staff resignations may rise.

Christina Maslach is a leading American researcher in the field of stress and has identified several key factors that contribute to anxiety felt by practitioners working with abused children:

- Issues around child abuse are always complex, with families suffering from multiple problems within society and in their personal relationships. It is hard to lay down rules which would apply across the board, as each case is unique.
- Statistics show that many childcare practitioners have themselves been the victims of abuse, and contact with abused children and their families may well trigger painful feelings and suppressed memories from childhood.

- In trying to help these families, you are exposed to people who are angry, despairing, suspicious, resentful and frustrated. They may well vent these feelings on you.
- Lack of resources, inadequate training and work overload make many long-term cases difficult to deal with.
- Rules of confidentiality may have to be set aside in the interests of the child and this can create a conflict of interest.

Regular training in child protection issues and the opportunity to discuss your feelings and practice with your line manager will help you maintain a professional distance.

Dealing with stress

Caring for a child who needs protection may create a great deal of stress. It is in the best interest of the child that you are aware of the stress and know how to deal with it. All training for childcare practitioners will cover stress management. Unlike most stressful work situations, resigning from your post is not the answer. You have a professional duty to the child and the child must come first. There are various coping strategies that will help you to reduce the level of stress:

- Discuss the issues with your line manager or designated teacher openly and honestly, not attempting to disguise your feelings. Their experience may help you to recognise and learn to live with the strength of your feelings.
- A clear action plan agreed with your line manager will help you to feel more positive and reduce the uncertainties inherent in the situation.
- You may be fortunate enough to have access to personal counselling, where you can express your feelings and opinions. This is particularly important if you have been a victim of abuse or neglect in the past.
- It can be very helpful to talk through the situation with a close and trusted friend, but do not disclose the identity of the family or the child.
- Take some training in general stress management techniques or do child protection training that includes stress management.
- Remember you are there for all the children; try not to allow the needs of one child to dominate so that the others do not get a fair share of your time. Make your day as normal as possible.
- Try to leave the stress behind you in the workplace. Try to relax on your days off.
- Exercise regularly to relieve tension and discover a relaxation technique that works for you.

Activity
List the physical, psychological and behavioural indicators of stress. Check your answers with Appendix 2.

The many communication skills you acquire in your training will help you in all areas of your work as a childcare practitioner: with children, with parents and with colleagues. When protecting children, you need to be a particularly skilled listener, able to express yourself clearly in speech and writing to parents, colleagues and other professionals.

KEY TERMS

You need to know what these words and phrases mean:
> communication
> confidentiality
> coping strategies
> disclosure
> effective listening
> feelings
> giving evidence in court
> interviews
> leading questions
> professional duty
> record keeping
> social listening
> stress
> voice of the child

Resources

Burnard, P. (1992) *Communicate! A Communication Skills Guide for Health Care Worker*s. Edward Arnold, London.

Elliott, M. (1994) *Keeping Safe: A Practical Guide to Talking to Children*. Coronet, London.

Jay, A. and Jay, R. (2004) *Effective Presentation*, 3rd edn. Pitman, London.

Looker, T., *Teach Yourself Managing Stress*, Teach Yourself, 2003.

Petrie, P. (1989) *Communication with Children and Adults*. Edward Arnold, London.

Wilson, C. and Powell, M. (2001) *A Guide to Interviewing Children*. Routledge, London.

WEBSITE

www.victimsupport.org.uk

11 CURRENT ISSUES

> **This chapter covers:**
> - Bullying
> - Family abductions
> - Female genital mutilation
> - Paedophiles
> - Influence of the media
> - Exploitation of children
> - Medical experts
> - Registration of childcare practitioners

Worldwide there are many issues that cause concern over the continuing exploitation and abuse of children and young people. While bullying and Internet safety are of immediate relevance and something you might have to deal with fairly often, some of the other matters may seem remote, but as a person caring for young children you need to have an informed view of global problems.

Bullying

Dan Olweus, an expert in the prevention of bullying, defines bullying as involving:
- deliberate hostility and aggression towards the victim;
- a victim who is weaker and less powerful than the bully or bullies;
- an outcome which is always painful and distressing to the victim.

In his book *Protecting Children*, Ben Whitney defines bullying as:
- actual or threatened violence;
- extortion of money or property;
- coercing a child into doing something they do not want to do;
- ignoring or shutting out a child from friendship groups;
- teasing and humiliating;
- picking on a child who is different;
- racist name-calling and making offensive remarks;
- offensive text messaging;
- spreading untrue rumours and gossip;
- sending insulting emails.

Bullying can be physical, verbal, emotional, racist and/or sexual. In its extreme form, it can lead to suicide in young people and is the main cause for school refusal. It can result in emotional scars which remain for life. Few schoolchildren

Bullying can cause long-lasting emotional scars

escape coming into contact with a bully during their schooldays. Children who bully and seek power over others have problems similar to those of abusive parents and need help and understanding.

Since the 1990s there has been increasing concern about bullying and the effect it has on children and their development. It has not always been seen as abuse, unless the effect on the child or the bullying is extreme. *Bullying: Don't Suffer in Silence* was published in 2000 by the Department for Education and Skills (DfES) and the Tell Someone campaign was launched in September 2003. Since 2003 all schools are required by law to have an anti-bullying policy. The DfES has helped by providing detailed information packs, videos and online resources.

Since 1998 over a thousand schools have been involved with the CHIPS programme offered by Childline that includes training programmes, conferences, newsletters and direct work with pupils. CHIPS stands for ChildLine in Partnership with Schools.

To think about

As a childcare practitioner, how would you manage a situation in a playground where a 7-year-old is taunting a younger child with racist comments?

The child who is bullied may show few physical signs, although they may have scratches, cuts and bruises that they are reluctant to explain. The bully will often pick on a particular child who may be different in some way, either physically such as having poor coordination or speech and language difficulties, or culturally such as belonging to a different ethnic or religious group than the majority of pupils.

In recent years a new form of bullying has emerged. Children and young people may be bullied online, via email and via text messaging. This can have far reaching affects as a child may feel they are being bullied within their own home and wherever they go, not just when they are in the vicinity of the bullies. Children may feel as though there is no escape. This is a worrying development. (Also see pages 168–70.)

To think about

Why do some children bully others? How can you help the bully in the infant school to recognise and stop this hurtful behaviour?

Bullying is rare among under-5s but it can still occur, even though they are usually well supervised at all times. Some forms of bullying may occur in an infant school, such as name-calling, fighting, excluding a child from their peer group, refusing to associate with them, and racial abuse. Staff who supervise the playground need to be aware that bullying can take place in areas that are not always in public view. Bullying may also occur in the lavatories, on the way to and from school, on the bus and in the park.

One school has its playground in a central courtyard. To combat bullying, there are friendship stations where children can go if they have no one to play with. The children take turns in being a friendship monitor and will help the friendless child find a friend. According to the school, this shows children a way of caring for others.

To think about

Look back on your schooldays. Were there any times when you were bullied? How did you feel? Did you ever become a bully yourself? Why do you think that was?

There are some behavioural indicators in children under 8 years old. Children who are bullied may be:
- reluctant or refusing to attend school or nursery;
- saying they feel unwell in the mornings;
- coming home with torn clothes;
- hungry, having had their lunch stolen;
- withdrawn, unhappy or showing signs of poor self-esteem;

- crying frequently and waking with nightmares;
- aggressive or starting to bully other children;
- reluctant to talk about what is happening to them.

A recent article in a newspaper suggested that many captains of industry had been bullies at school, treading ruthlessly on the feelings and hopes of other people in their pursuit of power and achievement. Kidscape research showed that bullies grow into adults who are four times more likely to end up in prison and to perpetrate domestic violence. The UK's first anti-bullying week began on 23 November 2004. Children who were against bullying wore wristbands. An advertising campaign featured many celebrities who had been bullied as children.

CHILDREN WHO ABUSE CHILDREN

During the 1990s there has been increasing concern about children who are violent towards each other, sometimes causing death. James Bulger was 2 years old when he was enticed away from a shopping centre by two boys aged 9 and 10; they tied him up and stoned him to death on a railway line. A young girl was killed by three other female teenagers at a fair. Children have also attacked and killed adults, as in the stabbing of Philip Lawrence, head teacher of a London school, the gang rape and attempted killing of an Austrian tourist, and the attack and murder of a barman who survived the Soho bombing.

Of equal concern to childcare practitioners is the sexual abuse of children by other children. Reporting in 1992, a committee of inquiry set up by NCH Action for Children found that up to 1 in 3 abusers were under age 18. A treatment centre at the Tavistock Clinic in London reported working with 76 children. Children as young as 8 were assessed and the clinic receives enquiries relating to children as young as 4. Some 91% of the abusers have been abused themselves, three-quarters of them sexually. It was suggested that many of the children may have been exposed to pornographic material. With many young perpetrators, sexual abuse is a way of bullying younger siblings. Some do not seem to comprehend that the abuse is sexual and appear to have very little sexual knowledge.

In 2000 an NSPCC survey asked 3 000 people aged between 18 and 24 about their childhood experiences. It showed that 43% of children who had suffered sexual abuse said that it had been committed by a brother or stepbrother, compared with 19% who named their stepfather and 14% who named their father. Evidence from NSPCC workers in the Midlands, where 70 young people are referred for treatment each year, showed that abusers are mainly boys aged 10–14 and their victims are mostly five years younger. Most of the abusers have themselves been victims of physical abuse. There are now specialist services that help children who are abusing, such as the Sexualised Inappropriate Behaviours Service (SIBS) in Warwickshire and the NCH service Ark.

To think about
What do you think is the main motivation behind children sexually abusing other children? What would you see as normal sexual experimentation?

It is very difficult for the general public and many professional people to comprehend and believe that children can be sexually abusive towards one another, but failure to acknowledge it will result in many more children suffering abuse.

Family abductions

The removal of a child by one parent without the consent of the other is an extremely distressing experience for the child and the parent who loses the child. Since 1995 the UK has seen a doubling in child abductions. The number of children involved in these cases appears to be growing as a result of:

- cheaper and more accessible global travel;
- abductors relying on the complicity of family and friends;
- free movement of people in the European Union and the reduction of border controls;
- increased numbers of mixed marriages and relationships, without a clear understanding of the cultural and religious customs of the other partner;
- courts now making court orders defining residence only if it is better for the child than making no order.

Some child abductions remain a family secret. Women are afraid of bringing dishonour to the family by disobeying their husbands or being evicted from their homes, which many share with their in-laws.

In the UK, parents who are married share parental responsibility for their child, including the decision about where the child should live. The law does not require them to consult each other in exercising their parental responsibility. Each may act alone. It is within the law for a married parent to remove a child from the home without the consent of the other parent, providing they do not remove the child abroad.

Where there is disagreement between parents, an application can be made to the court for a residence order stating where the child should live, or possibly an injunction preventing one parent removing the child from the care of the other. The same circumstances apply to divorced couples where no court order has been made. When a couple is in a partnership rather than a marriage, the father will have parental responsibility only if there is a parental responsibility agreement with the mother, a parental responsibility under Section 4 of the Children Act, or a residence order. Unless any of the above circumstances exist, it is unlawful for an unmarried father to remove the child from the mother.

If you are working in an establishment, you need to be extremely careful to hand over the children in your care only to named and known carers, with the authority of the parent. Never allow a child to go with a person you have doubts about, however plausible they may appear. Pages 162–3 shows a typical form to complete when a child starts a day nursery.

DAY NURSERY START FORM

1 Medical details

(i)   Please give details of your child's vaccination programme:

(ii) Please give details of any infectious diseases and child ailments:

(iii) Please give details of allergies, any allergic condition, or food intolerance:

(iv) Please give details of any serious illness that your child may have had, to include any hospital admissions:

(v)   Any further or other information which may be significant to your child's health and welfare:

2 Doctor's name:
Address:

Telephone:

3 Health visitor's name:
Address:

Telephone:

4 Social worker's name:
Address:

Telephone:

5 Consent for administration of drugs
I/we give my/our consent for the administration of basic first aid treatment (no prescribed medicines) to be given to my/our child/children by the nursery staff; and also for my/our child/children to be treated in hospital in an emergency, at the doctor's discretion.

I/we will not allow my/our child/children to be administered the following drug(s) or treatment(s) under any circumstances:

Full name of child (CAPITALS):

Signed: (Parent or legal guardian)

Date:

6 Permission to take child off premises

I/we hereby give permission for my/our child to be taken off the premises under the supervision of a responsible member of nursery staff:

Full name of child (CAPITALS):

Signed (by parent or legal guardian):

7 Emergency contacts

Please provide names and addresses of 2 people other than yourself or your partner, who we can contact in an emergency if we are unable to contact either parent/guardian.

(i) Name:

Relationship to child if any:

Daytime contact number:

(ii) Name:

Relationship to child if any:

Daytime contact number:

8 Name(s) of any person(s) allowed to collect your child:

NB: Anyone not named here will be refused access to your child unless we have received confirmation from you or your partner in person.

9 Name(s) of any person(s) NOT allowed to collect your child:

10 Declaration

I/we have read the regulations governing the admission of children to the Day Nursery and I/we agree to conform to and comply with these regulations.

Signature(s) of parent/guardian:

Date:

If you are working in a private home and one parent fears the child may be abducted by the other one, you should advise the parent to:

- encourage the separated parent to remain part of the child's life, keeping in touch by letter and telephone, giving the parent regular information about the child's progress and development;
- seek counselling and support services;
- seek a court order containing a restriction against removal;
- make sure the child is always accompanied when away from home;
- keep all important information concerning the child in a safe, accessible place as quick action might be needed in an emergency – important information

might include up-to-date photographs of children and parents, copies of court orders, full details of the child's passport, telephone numbers of the police and the solicitor, and full details of the potential abductor;

- consult a solicitor with specific expertise;
- keep the child's passport in a safe place such as a bank or a solicitor's office;
- prevent the other parent obtaining a birth certificate by contacting St Catherine's House in London;
- arrange for contact visits to be supervised and avoid allowing the child to leave the country on a contact visit.

To think about
Do you think marriage between two people from different countries, with conflicting belief systems, is usually successful?

The Hague Convention and the European Convention secured the return of the child to the child's country of habitual residence so that disputes can be resolved by the courts. There is no requirement under the conventions that the welfare of the child is paramount, and the merits of the case are not examined. Most non-European countries do not adhere to the Hague Convention, and where a child is abducted to a country that is not subject to the conventions, proceedings will have to be started in that country. This is a complex area, so seek further advice if you become involved.

FORCED MARRIAGES

About 250 cases of forced marriages are reported to the Foreign and Commonwealth Office each year. In a forced marriage one or both of the spouses do not consent to the marriage and some element of duress is involved. Most cases involve young women and girls from the age of 13, although a study has reported that up to 15% of the victims may be male. Forced marriage cannot be justified on religious grounds; every major faith condemns it and freely given consent is required of all major faiths. Reunite International Child Abduction Centre reports that children taken back to the parents' country of origin and often forced to marry accounted for 43% of child abduction cases in 2001.

Although it is not a criminal offence to force someone to marry within England and Wales, a number of criminal offences may be committed, including:
- threatening behaviour;
- assault;
- kidnap;
- abduction and/or imprisonment;
- rape.

The outcomes of a forced marriage may be:
- isolation;
- self-harm and attempted suicide;

- eating disorders;
- depression;
- poor attendance, motivation and performance at school or work;
- withdrawal from school;
- low self-esteem;
- limited career choices or not being allowed to work.

Female genital mutilation

In 2004 Amnesty International posted on its website a report about female genital mutilation (FGM) and its prevalence throughout the world. Here is a quotation from its report:

Female genital mutilation (FGM) is the term used to refer to the removal of part, or all, of the female genitalia. The most severe form is infibulation, also known as pharaonic circumcision. An estimated 15% of all mutilations in Africa are infibulations. The procedure consists of clitoridectomy (where all, or part of, the clitoris is removed), excision (removal of all, or part of, the labia minora), and cutting of the labia majora to create raw surfaces, which are then stitched or held together in order to form a cover over the vagina when they heal. A small hole is left to allow urine and menstrual blood to escape. In some less conventional forms of infibulation, less tissue is removed and a larger opening is left.

The vast majority (85%) of genital mutilations performed in Africa consist of clitoridectomy or excision. The least radical procedure consists of the removal of the clitoral hood.

In some traditions a ceremony is held, but no mutilation of the genitals occurs. The ritual may include holding a knife next to the genitals, pricking the clitoris, cutting some pubic hair, or light scarification in the genital or upper thigh area.

An estimated 135 million of the world's girls and women have undergone genital mutilation, and two million girls a year are at risk of mutilation – approximately 6,000 per day. It is practised extensively in Africa and is common in some countries in the Middle East. It also occurs, mainly among immigrant communities, in parts of Asia and the Pacific, North and Latin America and Europe.

FGM is reportedly practised in more than 28 African countries. There are no figures to indicate how common FGM is in Asia. It has been reported among Muslim populations in Indonesia, Sri Lanka and Malaysia, although very little is known about the practice in these countries. In India a small Muslim sect, the Daudi Bohra, practise clitoridectomy.

In the Middle East, FGM is practised in Egypt, Oman, Yemen and the United Arab Emirates.

There have been reports of FGM among certain indigenous groups in central and south America, but little information is available.

In industrialised countries, genital mutilation occurs predominantly among immigrants from countries where mutilation is practised. It has been reported in Australia, Canada, Denmark, France, Italy, the Netherlands, Sweden, the UK and

the US. Girls or girl infants living in industrialized countries are sometimes oper-
ated on illegally by doctors from their own community who are resident there. More
frequently, traditional practitioners are brought into the country or girls are sent
abroad to be mutilated. No figures are available on how common the practise is
among the populations of industrialised countries.

© *Amnesty International 2004*

THE ROLE OF THE CHILDCARE PRACTITIONER

Women who have undergone genital mutilation are often more likely to wish their own daughters to suffer this procedure, seeing it as culturally correct and in their daughters' best interests. Childcare practitioners should be alert to the possibility of mutilation when working with members from a community known to practise genital mutilation extensively, and the risk is higher if elderly female relatives are part of the family group.

Mutilation may occur from the first week of birth up to age 12 using a variety of implements, frequently unsterilised, and without anaesthesia. The practice has been illegal in the UK since 1985, and from March 2004 it has been unlawful to take girls abroad for FGM, with prison sentences of 5 to 14 years. It is believed there are 74 000 first-generation African immigrants in the UK who have undergone FGM and up to 7 000 girls under age 16 in these communities who are at risk from the procedure.

FGM may result in serious health risks to the child, including shock, urine retention, tetanus, loss of blood and pelvic infection as well as infertility and complications during pregnancy and childbirth. Countries practising FGM consider Western countries to be racist in their disapproval of FGM. In the UK anyone involved in multidisciplinary child protection work has a duty to work in partnership with the parents as long as it is consistent with the child's welfare and they have a duty to address issues concerning race and gender that could affect how a child might best be helped. Legal steps must be taken to prevent a child being mutilated and social workers may seek an emergency protection order or a 'prohibited steps' order to prevent the child being sent out of the country. If it is impossible to dissuade the parents from mutilating the child, child protection procedures might be invoked.

Paedophiles

Paedophiles sexually abuse children. They are sexually attracted to young children below the age of sexual consent. This is a compulsive pattern of behaviour and they do not see the need to stop molesting children. They come from all classes, professions, races and religions and are male and female, but the vast majority are male. They are not immediately identifiable as they keep their sexual life secret. Most of them are not strangers to the children but are part of their family or community.

In May 1997 a paedophile ring was discovered composed of members of St John Ambulance, people usually regarded as trustworthy. Paedophiles can be any member of the general population and are only identified after disclosure or discovery. They prey mainly on children they know and often go to great lengths to get on good terms with a particular family. They attempt to infiltrate games clubs for children or to make themselves indispensable to schools. Single-parent families are particularly vulnerable as the mothers can become isolated and lonely, and the children may not have a male role model living at home.

The term 'grooming' is used to describe the way a paedophile uses routines that become rituals to build a relationship to gain a child's trust, isolate the child from protecting adults and provide opportunities for the abuse to take place. Paedophiles often take time to lead children through a progression of activities from 'innocent' cuddling to an introduction to pornography, and finally to sexual activity using different ways of ensuring that the child remains silent. Your suspicions might be aroused if someone from outside the family is taking too close an interest in a child in your care and the child appears to be uneasy in their presence, or even shows signs or behavioural indicators of abuse.

The NSPCC suggests that children are rarely picked at random and that paedophiles are skilled at identifying vulnerable children. They may target a child who is:

- too trusting;
- seeking love or affection;
- lonely or bereaved;
- lacking in confidence;
- bullied;
- disabled or unable to communicate well;
- in care or away from home;
- already a victim of abuse;
- eager to succeed in activities, such as sport or other interests, which may allow the child to be manipulated by a potential abuser.

Other research has suggested that poverty might be a factor.

In September 1997 the sex offenders register was established to enable the police to track and supervise paedophiles and to check on potential childcare employees with unsupervised access to young children. Unfortunately, this did not include paedophiles who have not been convicted, such as Ian Huntley, the school caretaker who abused and murdered two young girls in Cambridgeshire in 2003. The register requires sex offenders who, after 1 September 1997, were convicted or cautioned, were serving a custodial or community sentence, or were being supervised, to notify the police of their names and addresses and of any subsequent changes. This requirement lasts for varying periods of time according to the seriousness of the offence but is a lifetime requirement for anyone imprisoned for 30 months or more. Less than half the known paedophiles have registered their names and addresses with the police, even though discovery will lead to a heavy fine and/or imprisonment.

Sex offender orders will be applied to offenders who have been convicted or cautioned for a sexual offence if their behaviour continues to pose a threat. It will also apply to offenders who have been convicted abroad. The order enables the courts to impose conditions such as preventing offenders from loitering near schools and playgrounds. It will remain in force for a minimum of five years and requires that the person concerned is also subject to the registration provisions of the Sex Offenders Act, if they are not already subject, for the duration of the order.

Following the sexual assault, kidnapping and killing of a child named Megan, the US state of New Jersey passed a law requiring courts to inform local people when a convicted sex offender is released or paroled into their community. This campaign became a national crusade, and 41 states have followed New Jersey, invoking what has become known as Megan's law. In the UK, after the killing of 8-year-old Sarah Payne in 2000, a similar campaign was started by the *News of the World* newspaper to allow parents controlled access to the sex offenders register. This has not happened in the UK because:

- sex offenders simply change their address;
- media hype has caused confusion in some people's minds and the establishment of vigilante groups;
- vigilantes can drive paedophiles underground.

Megan's law has done nothing to protect children in the US, and the number of children killed there has continued to rise.

To think about
Do you think general access to the sex offenders register contravenes civil liberties?

The number of convictions against sex offenders remains worryingly low. Experts estimate that less than 1 in 50 sexual offences results in a criminal conviction. It is thought that more effort is required into gathering and analysing information about abusers and the scale of abuse so that effective prevention, early intervention and treatment can be provided.

THE INTERNET

The Internet is used by millions of people worldwide and offers widening horizons and new educational opportunities to children and their families. Unfortunately, it has also given paedophiles access to each other, and some of the messages relayed are most disturbing, presenting images of children engaged in sexual activity. Growing numbers of babies and toddlers are involved, possibly because they are unable to pass on any information, and are being abused in ever more revolting ways. Several studies show a definite link between possessing and collecting child abuse images and being involved in abusing children, with up to one-third of those arrested being involved in hands-on abuse.

In 2002 an American investigation into child pornography websites led to the establishment of Operation Ore in the UK, where it was found that 7 300 Britons had accessed hardcore child pornography. The inquiry started by investigating 1 400 suspects whose work gave them access to children, including care workers, teachers, doctors, scout leaders, social workers and suspected and convicted pae-dophiles. Further investigations were made into the criminal justice system. At least one magistrate, several prison and probation officers and police officers were charged, and 50 policemen were arrested. The third and largest category of suspects consisted of those without criminal records or links with children and included businessmen, civil servants, rock stars and many others leading seem-ingly respectable lives. It will take many years to complete this operation, due to the resources available and the cost of the undertaking.

Very few of the children used in the videos have been identified, often because they are being abused by a family member and are too frightened to come forward. It has been found that even when children were too young to realise what was happening at the time, taking part in these videos has affected them emotionally in later life and adversely affected their relationships.

There is much debate about the need to exercise more control over the content of images on the Internet, and it is hoped legislation will shortly be in place to deal with this problem. The government's Internet task force on child protection is developing a child safety agenda and more coordinated police action is planned. A warning by NCH Action for Children stated that children can stumble accidentally on pictures of explicit material. A software company has developed Safety-Net, which identifies and prevents specific types of pictures and words or access to certain Internet groups.

Chat rooms

Parents and teachers have become aware of the dangers inherent in chat rooms and have exercised 'parental control software' over many such sites. In November 2004 a 31-year-old man pleaded guilty to having 'cybersex' with a 13-year-old girl. He pretended he was 19 and used a live webcam link to watch her pose naked. She saw him using lewd and indecent practices. He was arrested and the case made legal history as until then it had been assumed the abuser had to be in the same place as their victim.

The fact that chat rooms are known to be dangerous places has appealed to some children who enjoy taking risks, and younger children certainly need shielding from these dangers. In 2004 the Home Office produced an excellent booklet entitled *Keep Your Child Safe on the Internet*.

The government's task force on child protection on the Internet offers the following advice:

- Tell children to treat strangers they meet on the net with the same caution they would apply in real life.
- Do not divulge personal details and do not arrange offline meetings without parental supervision.
- Discourage children from entering into private one-on-one conversations in chat rooms. They are safer when a conversation is in full view.
- Encourage children to tell you about negative experiences they encounter online. Reassure them it is not their fault and that they will not be banned from the net for doing so.
- Make a favourite folder of mutually agreed sites that your child can visit; they could include child-friendly chat rooms.

Children do not know the dangers of believing information given to them in chat rooms

- Ask your Internet service provider (ISP) about its safety features.
- Report any attempted contact by suspected paedophiles to the police. Any illegal material can be reported to the Internet Watch Foundation on 08456 008844.

A study by the University of Central Lancashire in 2003 found that 1 in 4 children attended face-to-face meeting with strangers they had come into contact with in Internet chat rooms, compared with 1 in 10 in 2002. The survey of children aged 8–11 found that 60% did not know about the dangers of believing all the information given to them in the chat rooms compared with 30% in 2002. Rachel O'Connell, the study's author, believes the government's campaign may have backfired by appealing to children's sense of risk. Software packages are available to screen Internet material.

The influence of the media

The media includes newspapers, books and magazines; television and radio; theatre, cinema and video; computers and the Internet. Newspapers have always played a role in keeping the general public informed and educated about child protection issues. In 1996 and 1997 investigative journalism unveiled abuse in children's residential homes in Merseyside and Wales. Many of the children who were abused in the past committed suicide, while others have found their lives ruined. The publicity has led to government action to tighten standards in children's homes.

Journalists become interested in child abuse matters when the numbers of children abused are very large, when the perpetrator is well known, or when the abuse of an individual child results in death. It was the media's attention to the death of Maria Colwell, and more recently Victoria Climbié, that focused the general public's attention and pushed forward changes in practice.

Journalists sometimes seem to enjoy pointing out the failure of authorities and social workers and their reporting is often one-sided. Nevertheless, the media has contributed a great deal to the progress made over the past quarter-century to ensure the systems for protecting children are now more effective. It is difficult to achieve a balance between the right to privacy and the public's right to know. Preserving confidentiality in the traditional sense can contribute to the preservation of the family 'secret'. The use of surveillance video cameras in hospital paediatric wards has revealed instances of abuse by parents.

Television, plays and films often attract large audiences when depicting an episode of child abuse. Abusers are sometimes shown in a sympathetic light, and the general public may gain some understanding of the factors which lead to abuse. A good example is the televising of the Louise Woodward case. Her conviction for murder was changed to manslaughter and her sentence was reduced, possibly due to the sympathy aroused by the coverage.

Pornographic videos that are carelessly left around or deliberately shown to children expose them to films which may show sex in a sadistic or bestial way; this may disturb children and have a negative influence on their behaviour.

Exploitation of children

CHILD PROSTITUTION

History shows us that children have always been exploited and this continues to be the case.

Prostitution is defined as the provision of sexual services in exchange for some form of payment, which may range from money, drink or drugs to goods or provision of a basic need, such as shelter or food. In November 2004 the Children's Society estimated that over 5 000 people less than 18 years of age are involved in prostitution in the UK; many have run away from home or from local authority care and have nowhere safe to go.

Child prostitution includes boys and girls under the age of 18. Guidance issued by the Department of Health states that young people involved in prostitution should be regarded as victims of abuse. Children who constantly return to prostitution, particularly those aged 16 and 17, can be prosecuted. The factors that can lead to child prostitution include:

■ poverty and gaps in the benefit system may lead to homelessness and family conflict, and ultimately to child prostitution;

- increasing family break-ups and reconstituted family structures which sometimes lead to emotionally damaged children, often starved of affection at home and subsequently taken into care;
- abused children;
- inadequate sex education policies;
- inadequate social policies to ensure that children in care are properly supervised and protected;
- drug and alcohol abuse;
- the law relating to pimps and clients of under-age prostitutes appears to discriminate against the children rather than the adults;
- the notion of life in a big city may appeal to young immature people, who then become trapped by adults preying on them.

In July 2004 the government issued *Paying the Price*, a consultation paper aimed at overhauling prostitution laws; its three key areas are prevention, protection and support, and justice. Much of this paper is aimed at safeguarding children. The Children's Society's 'Safe and Sound' campaign is calling for a national network of safe emergency accommodation for young runaways under 16.

Sex tourism

UNICEF, the United Nations Children's Fund, recently estimated that 1 million children worldwide are reportedly forced into the sex market annually. The first world congress against the commercial sexual exploitation of children was held in Sweden in 1996 and a second congress was held in Japan in 2001. The priorities they identified were the need for stronger penalties for those using or profiting from under-age sex workers plus improved education to change attitudes in local communities and law enforcement agencies.

One major problem is the estimated 40 million children born each year who are not recorded or registered at birth. In some countries the law protects girls from rape but not boys. There are several countries notorious for exploiting children for sex, particularly Thailand, the Philippines and Sri Lanka, and an expanding tourist industry has seen the growth in tourists travelling to these countries and others for sexual gratification with young children. These activities have seen an increase in the incidence of HIV and AIDS, and in the numbers of children being born who do not receive financial support from their fathers.

Natural disasters, such as the tsunami that occurred on 26 December 2004, left many children homeless and orphaned. There was considerable concern that these children would be abducted and sold into the sex trade. End Child Prostitution, Pornography and Trafficking (ECPAT) says that for many child sex workers there is no happy ending. The most that can be done is to help them get greater protection from the men who exploit them, or to provide them with better health care.

Save the Children has warned of a worldwide expansion of the child sex industry and of the global sexual exploitation of children by paedophiles and criminal gangs. Increasing numbers of children are becoming involved, not only in prostitution but also in child trafficking and pornography. Poverty is identified as a critical factor in the growth of the child sex industry. This is a global issue; it happens in Britain and in many other countries. Save the Children recently produced the report *Kids for Hire*.

Part 2 of the Sex Offenders Act 1997 gives UK courts jurisdiction to prosecute those who travel abroad to have sex with children. The Offences (Conspiracy and Incitement) Act 1996 allows courts to try those who organise trips abroad for child abusers. In February 2005 the Foreign Office and UK police began a joint initiative to help South-east Asian countries combat the child sex trade and to catch British paedophiles abroad.

CHILD EMPLOYMENT

In the UK an estimated 2 million children between the ages of 10 and 16 have a part-time job; the main areas of employment are:

■ family businesses;
■ newspaper rounds;
■ shop work;
■ cleaning;
■ babysitting;
■ running errands.

All these jobs teach children responsibility and independence, but the danger is that the children are exploited by being paid very little and are expected to work too many hours, impairing their ability to concentrate, make progress at school and enjoy their childhood. In some jobs they may be at risk through lack of training or lack of health and safety provision.

Studies appear to indicate that children and families are not aware of the laws concerning child employment. The Children and Young Persons Act 1933 controls the age at which they can start working, the number of hours they can work and the types of jobs they can do. Enforcement of the law is the responsibility of the local authority's education welfare officers.

Employment in other countries

UNICEF recently reported that some 250 million children under the age of 15 have to work in dangerous, unacceptable conditions, mostly in Asia, Africa and Latin America. The true figure could be much higher as most of the work is unseen and unreported. In some countries the high incidence of HIV and AIDS has left many children orphaned. The report describes many of the risks, including:

■ inhaling pesticides;
■ undertaking heavy manual labouring;
■ exposure to snake and insect bites.

It calls for free compulsory primary education in developing countries.

Some of the goods sold in the UK are made by children held in virtual slavery in factories abroad. The International Labour Organisation (ILO) faces the gigantic task of organising governments, employers and trade unions to secure agreements of industry-wide standards that prevent exploitation of children and 'ban other employment practices which are incompatible with human rights and labour standards'.

In some countries children work in poor conditions in factories for slave wages

In June 2003 UNICEF launched its UK campaign End Child Exploitation. This has gone some way to highlighting the exploitation of children in the developing world.

Activity
There are many forms of exploitation. Research the sale, trafficking and abduction of children. Find out about the use of children in medical research.

Child actors and models
Although most children who model or act are well protected by a sensible family and by the agencies, there have been cases where children are exploited in an explicitly sexual way. In the US there are competitions held for very young children, from the age of 3, who are trained to perform for an adult audience in a pseudo-mature way. The competitions are held all over the country. In one case, a child was raped and murdered in very suspicious circumstances and the murderer has still not been charged. Even if no significant harm comes to children, some argue that they lose a valuable part of their childhood.

THE DANGERS OF RESIDENTIAL CARE

When children have been abused and the courts decide that they need a place of safety, they may be placed in residential care. This is not always such a safe place. In December 1996 the *Independent* newspaper reported that police had launched a full-scale investigation into allegations of sexual and physical abuse in children's homes in Merseyside, north-west England. Around 3 000 children were thought to have been involved in 15 homes. The allegations of abuse stretched back over 20 years. The abuse was thought to be systematic, involving paedophile activity, with children being moved between homes.

The following year, the same newspaper reported on another major abuse inquiry: many hundreds of children were alleged to have been sexually abused in children's homes across North Wales, involving many staff and six police officers. The role of the council's insurers in North Wales was also to be investigated, as it was further alleged that it was these insurers who caused the council to turn a blind eye to what was going on, as any inquiry would be too expensive.

To think about
Is it safer to leave some abused children at home, as the risk of putting them into residential care might be greater? What would be the best care for some of these children?

The £6 million public inquiry of the North Wales case was chaired by Sir William Utting. It showed that 650 children were physically and sexually abused and that up to 80 staff were involved. Social services were criticised for being, at the very least, careless about the plight of many children in their care, or at worst, negligent to the point of gross professional incompetence, or even guilty of 'closing their eyes'. The Utting Report urged the government to regulate private foster care, bring small homes into line with larger ones, set up a specialist group to develop a childcare strategy for residential care, and be more vigilant in checking the backgrounds of potential employees.

A similar scandal in Cheshire is thought to involve more than 4 000 children, and in Clwyd six care workers were jailed for offences against children. Other types of abuse have been reported; one of them is 'pin down'. This is where children are confined to their rooms for long periods without any contact with other people. Once recommended for unruly children, pin down has now been shown to be cruel.

There are obviously many well-run homes that do a good job. Most of the children who live in residential homes have experienced trauma and emotional deprivation in their own families, and they deserve the quality of care enjoyed by most children in supportive families. They must be protected from further abuse. In 2004 there were 5 000 children living in the UK without their parents, and half the children in care were asylum seekers.

One of the problems is that, despite requirements for disclosure of criminal background and police checks, some sex offenders are clever and persuasive enough to gain employment time and again with young and vulnerable children.

Many local authorities now prefer to place children in foster care instead of residential care, but this too has its dangers, for the child and the foster family. The foster carers need to be selected and vetted very carefully, and will require training and support. Older foster children in the family, who have been abused themselves, have been known to abuse younger children in the foster family. Not all foster parents have the emotional resources themselves to cope with very disturbed unhappy children.

> ## To think about
> Consider the adoption of children from abroad. Does the adoption of a child living in dire circumstances in one country justify raising the child in another country and culture?

THE EFFECTS OF WAR ON CHILDREN

Many regimes conscript young children into the army — the war in Rwanda enlisted many thousands. Even when wars appear to be over, the damaging after-effects can last for decades. Some countries use systematic forced conscription of children. UNICEF recently stated that 2 million children have been killed in global wars in the past decade, and the situation is worsening. Up to 5 million children have been disabled, some by landmines; 1 million are orphaned or separated from their parents; and some 10 million are psychologically traumatised by war. Most children who die are not killed by bombs or bullets but succumb to starvation or sickness.

STREET CHILDREN

The term 'street children' refers to children for whom the street has become their real home, more so than their family. Most are homeless and orphaned. They live in situations where there is no protection, supervision or direction from responsible adults. They are found in many of the poorest countries of the world, particularly South America. In Brazil and Columbia, police frequently 'clean up' the streets by murdering as many of these children as they can find. Street children everywhere face constant violence and abuse. We should not be complacent about street children in the UK, as many runaways congregate in big cities and are at risk of exploitation, pornography, prostitution and drug trafficking.

Many runaway children end up living on the streets

Medical experts

Medical practitioners are abandoning child protection work for fear they will be vilified or not believed if they report parents they suspect of harming their children. Below is an extract from an article in the *Sunday Herald* (9 May 2004).

Research carried out by Professor Robert Carpenter and colleagues at the London School of Hygiene and Tropical Medicine suggests that 2 or 3 cot deaths in a family should not automatically arouse suspicion of infanticide. They reviewed the deaths of babies under 1 year old in families that had already experienced a cot death and were enrolled on the Care of Next Infant support programme. Of the 6 373 babies on the programme, 57 died. They report that 9 of these deaths were inevitable and 48 were unexpected. Two families lost 2 children and 44 lost one. The data suggests that second deaths are not very rare and that the majority (80–90%) are natural.

TESTIMONY OF CHILD ABUSE EXPERTS UNDER NEW SCRUTINY

Two massive investigations into the court testimony of expert witnesses in British child abuse cases have been launched amid fears that children have been returned to abusive households on flawed evidence.

The unprecedented reviews, to be co-ordinated by the Royal College of Paediatrics and Child Health, will examine the scientific basis of theories put forward in court cases. It will be the first time that the opinions of witnesses in child abuse cases will effectively be 'peer reviewed' to establish their reliability.

The first, involving more than 50 eminent US paediatricians, will examine the transcripts of recent high-profile child abuse cases to review the quality of evidence given by expert witnesses on both sides. The study aims to lead to better quality witnesses in the wake of the recent cases of Angela Cannings, Sally Clark, Trupti Patel and Mark Latta – all were acquitted of murdering their children.

A second review – to be chaired by the Scottish paediatrician Professor Neil McIntosh – will research every study that has been published in the area of physical abuse. A panel of six UK experts, including radiologists, neurosurgeons and pathologists, will produce a report which highlights the most reliable and up-to-date research on the subject. Another study by the group is to be launched into research relating to sexual abuse.

...

The Royal College had been approached by around 50 US paediatricians – led by Professor David Chadwick of the University of Utah – who were concerned that the 'British child protection procedures were in danger of breaking down'. The publicity of recent cases and the vilification of expert witnesses, such as Professor Sir Roy Meadow and Professor David Southall, two of the country's main experts on Munchausen's Syndrome by Proxy (MSBP), also known as Fabricated or Induced Illness.

Both Meadow and Southall were reported to the General Medical Council over concerns about their opinions and, Marcovitch says, this has led to a situation in the UK where MSBP is being discredited as an illness, despite widespread belief among medical experts that the condition does exist.

...

Chris Hobbs, a consultant paediatrician at St James's Hospital in Leeds, said: 'This area of work is now seen as a liability. It's very difficult to get young doctors into this line of work. We advertise but nobody wants to do the work. There is a real crisis.'

Hobbs, who has worked in the area of child protection for more than 20 years, believes there is evidence that doctors are increasingly practising 'defensive medicine' – not reporting cases which might involve abuse -- for fear of getting it wrong.

'They are also backing away from going to court as expert witnesses.'

From 'Testimony of child abuse experts under scrutiny.' *Sunday Herald* 9th May 2004.

Medical practitioners are leaving child protection work for fear of being criticised

Registration and inspection

All daycare providers in England caring for children under the age of eight years are registered and inspected by the Early Years Directorate within the Office for Standards in Education (Ofsted). Procedures for registration and inspection changed in 2007/2008. There are now two registers: the **Childcare Register** and the **Early Years Register**.

CHILDCARE REGISTER

This is a register of providers who are registered by Ofsted to care for children from birth to 17 years. The register has two parts:

- **The voluntary part**
  Providers who are not eligible for compulsory registration may choose to register here. These are mainly people looking after children aged eight and over, or providing care in the child's home (e.g. nannies).
- **The compulsory part**
  Providers must register if they care for one or more children following their fifth birthdays until they reach their eighth birthdays.

Registered settings must meet the Requirements of the Childcare Register at all times. Ofsted will carry out periodic inspections of settings to assess the standard of the provision, and will publish a public report which will be available to families using, or wishing to use, the provision. The Requirements fall into the categories below. An example of the content of each category is given here. You can see the requirements in full in the document *The Guide to Registration on the Childcare Register*, available on the Ofsted website (www.ofsted.gov.uk).

Welfare of the children being cared for
Example content of this category:
- Children receiving childcare are kept safe from harm.
- There must be a ratio of 1 adult to every 8 children.

Arrangements for safeguarding children
- There must be written child protection procedures.
- No one unsuitable to work with children has unsupervised access to a child.

Suitability of persons to care for, or be in regular contact with children
- There must be effective systems to ensure that those in contact with children are suitable to work with them.

Qualifications and training
- At least half of all persons caring for children have successfully completed a relevant qualification at a minimum of level 2.
- The manager has a relevant qualification at a minimum of level 3.

Suitability and safety of premises and equipment
- Premises and equipment used are safe and suitable for childcare.

How the childcare provision is organised
- Where older and younger children are together, the behaviour of children over the age of eight years does not have a negative effect on the younger children.
- Childcare is accessible and inclusive by taking all reasonable steps to ensure that the needs of each child are met.

Procedures for dealing with complaints
- Each complaint must be fully investigated.

Records to be kept
- Certain records must be kept and retained for a period of two years.

Providing information to parents
- Information about the activities the children will undertake is given.
- Copies of safeguarding procedures and complaints procedures are available.

Providing information to Ofsted
- Ofsted must be informed of changes of circumstance as soon as possible.

Changes to premises and provision
- Settings must inform Ofsted of a change to the address of the premises where they are providing childcare.

Changes to people
- The registered person must inform Ofsted of a change to their name, address or telephone number.

Matters affecting the welfare of children
- Ofsted must be informed of certain events, including incidents of food poisoning and any serious accidents or injuries to children.

Insurance
- The setting must be covered by insurance for death, injury, public liability, damage or other loss.

Certificate of registration
- The certificate of registration must be displayed.

All childcare providers must also comply with other relevant legislation including that covering health and safety, disability discrimination, food hygiene, fire and planning requirements.

Early Years Register

In addition, since 2008, all childcarers providing for children from birth to the 31 August following their fifth birthday must register on the Early Years Register and deliver the Early Years Foundation Stage (EYFS), which is a curriculum framework. You can find out more about the EYFS at www.standards.dfes.gov.uk/eyfs.

Childcarers and settings who are exempt from compulsory registration on the Childcare Register choose to join the voluntary part of the register so they can demonstrate to parents that they have met essential standards, including an enhanced CRB check (Criminal Records Bureau check). Ofsted makes registration checks before registration is granted, and once registered, childcarers will be regularly inspected. This reassures families about the welfare of their child.

In addition, in terms of the working tax credits and employer childcare vouchers, the voluntarily registered provider becomes "qualifying childcare." This enables parents eligible for the Government benefits to access them towards the cost of childcare. This is further encouragement for providers to apply to the voluntary register. (The voluntary part of the Childcare Register replaces the previous Childcare Approval Scheme.)

Conclusion

The world is still a dangerous place for children, but many laws are being passed and checks introduced. The difficulty is to do this without being too protective towards young people and to allow them sufficient independence to become the well-rounded and autonomous adults of tomorrow. Working with abused children is very demanding and very stressful. We hope that by writing this book we have clarified the issues and procedures that will help you contribute to the prevention of abuse and neglect, to recognise the signs and indicators of abuse, and to work fruitfully with the children and families who have been affected.

Resources

Buckingham, D. and Bragg, S. (2004) *Young People, Sex and the Media: The Facts of Life*. Palgrave, Basingstoke, Hants.

Calder, M. (2004) *Child Sexual Abuse and the Internet*. Russell House, Lyme Regis, Dorset.

Elliott, M. et al. (2001) *How to Stop Bullying*. Kidscape, London.

Kitzinger, J. (2004) *Framing Abuse*. Pluto Press, Andover, Hants.

Lavalette, M. (ed.) (1999) *A Thing of the Past? Child Labour in Britain*. Liverpool University Press, Liverpool.

O'Connell-Davidson, J. (2005) *Children in the Global Sex Trade*. Polity, Cambridge.

Rigby, K. (1996) *Bullying in Schools*. Jessica Kingsley, London.

Rigby, K. (2001) *Stop the Bullying*. Jessica Kingsley, London.

Schlemmer, B. (ed.) (2000) *The Exploited Child*. Zed Books, London.

Taylor, M. and Quayle, E. (2003) *Child Pornography*. Bruner Routledge, London.

WEBSITES

www.bullying.co.uk
www.reunite.org
www.parentinternational.com
www.amnesty.org
www.thinkuknow.co.uk
www.childnet-int.org
www.kidsmart.org.uk
www.chatdanger.com
www.nnspcc.org.uk/kidszone/surfingsafely
www.iwf.org.uk
www.wiredsafety.org
www.getnetwise.org
www.unicef.org.uk
www.child-soldiers.org
www.learningplanet.com
www.hrw.org/en/press

www.ecpat.org
www.bfms.org.uk

APPENDIX 1: CHRONOLOGY OF ACTS THAT AFFECT CHILDREN

1802 The Health and Morals of Apprentices Act restricted pauper cotton apprentices to 12 hours' work a day.

1833 The Factory Act limited the working hours of children in textile mills and appointed factory inspectors with a right of entry.

1872 The Infant Life Protection Act was a reaction to scandals resulting from baby farming, where mothers entrusted their children to women to be looked after for payment. Foster parents had to register with the local authority. An investigatory procedure into the deaths of infants was established. It was extended in 1897 to cover children up to age 5.

1872 The Bastardy Laws Amendment Act supported a mother's claim for maintenance from the putative father.

1874 Registration of births and deaths became compulsory.

1889 Following the inauguration of the National Society for the Prevention of Cruelty to Children (NSPCC), the Prevention of Cruelty to Children Act was passed specifically to protect children. This was essentially a criminal rather than a social welfare approach.

1889 The Poor Law (Children) Act gave boards of guardians the authority to assume parental rights over abandoned children. This was extended in 1899 to include orphans, children of parents who were disabled or in prison, or unfit to have care of them. In 1904 the responsibility was transferred from the Poor Law guardians to the local authority.

1904 The Prevention of Cruelty to Children Act gave the local authorities powers to remove children from their parents, including those who had not actually been convicted of a criminal offence against them, but where it met the needs of the children.

1906 The Education (Provision of Meals) Act gave the local authority the right to levy a rate to finance school meals for those in need. This followed a report in 1904 when attention was drawn to the poor physique of recruits in the Boer War, and concern was expressed about the lack of good food, good air and good clothes. The Act also required the setting up of children's care committees to look into the circumstances of children needing feeding. Schools for mothers were established, which later became infant welfare centres.

1906 Huddersfield promoted a private Act for compulsory notification of births within the borough.

1907 The Notification of Births Act gave similar powers to authorities that desired them. This became compulsory in 1915.

1907 The Education (Administrative Provisions) Act introduced medical inspection of children in elementary schools. It was the first personal health service to be established by Parliament.

1908 Concerned with the cases of cruelty and neglect, the Children Act attempted to strengthen the powers of the courts for the benefit of the child at risk. It established juvenile courts and borstals to deal with young offenders under the age of 16. Shopkeepers were forbidden to sell alcohol and tobacco to juveniles. Limits were set on the hours children were allowed to work.

1911 Maternity benefits were introduced.

1929 Infant Life (Preservation) Act.

1933 The Children and Young Persons Act was primarily concerned with treatment of young offenders but also included young people who were the victims of cruelty or other offences committed by adults. Local education authorities were now required to investigate such cases and bring them before a court empowered to commit the children to the care of the local authority. The emphasis was on rescue, not prevention.

1938 The Infanticide Act accepted the fact that some women may injure or kill their babies while suffering from severe mental illness associated with childbirth.

1948 The Children Act emphasised the importance of keeping children in the care of their natural family wherever possible. This was a shift from punishing bad parents to acting in the interests of the children. Children's departments were established, staffed by social workers known as childcare officers.

1963 The Children and Young Persons Act raised the age of criminal responsibility from 8 to 10. It enabled the local authorities to use resources, including money, to promote the welfare of the child.

1969 The Children and Young Persons Act increased the priority given to caring for children away from home.

1975 The Children Act and the Child Care Act 1980 both emphasised care in fostering and adoption.

1989 Children Act; see Chapters 1 and 5.

1994 Data Protection Act.

1996 Family Law Act.

1997 Sex Offenders Act.

1997 The Police Act.

1998 Human Rights Act; see Chapter 5.

1998 Data Protection Act.

1999 Protection of Children Act; see Chapter 1.

2000 The Care Standards Act led to national care standards for day-care and childminding.

2002 Education Act; see Chapter 6.

2002 The Adoption and Children Act. This replaced provisions of the outdated Adoption Act 1976, placing a duty on local authorities to provide adoption support services, and allowing single people, unmarried couples and same sex couples to adopt.

2004 Children Act; see Chapters 1 and 5.

2004 Domestic Violence Crime and Victims Act; see Chapter 2.

2006 The Childcare Act; see Chapter 1.

APPENDIX 2: INDICATORS OF STRESS

Physical

- Aches and pains
- Anorexia
- Headaches
- Dry mouth
- Nail biting
- Fatigue
- Tension
- Sexual dysfunction
- Fidgeting
- Insomnia
- Sweating
- Palpitations
- Back pain
- High blood pressure
- Nausea
- Restlessness
- Skin blotches or flushes
- Stomach cramps
- Lack of coordination
- Twitching
- Shaking
- Rapid breathing
- Diarrhoea
- Constipation
- Neck pain
- Rigid body
- Clenched hands
- Gritted teeth
- Little eye contact

Psychological

- Feeling anxious
- Feeling bored
- Feeling detached
- Feeling confused
- Feeling depressed
- Feeling helpless
- Feeling lethargic
- Feeling lonely
- Feeling negative
- Feeling nervous
- Feeling angry
- Feeling defensive
- Feeling rejected
- Feeling isolated
- Feeling indecisive
- Feeling tearful
- Experiencing mood swings
- Experiencing paranoia
- Experiencing lack of concentration
- Experiencing nightmares
- Experiencing lack of self-control

Behavioural

- Overeating
- Undereating
- Increased drinking
- Increased smoking
- Irritable
- Fidgeting
- Violent outbursts
- Waking early
- Unable to organise time
- Unsociable behaviour
- Aggressive
- Cynical
- Finding fault
- Crying
- Inflexible
- Isolated
- Low sex drive
- Nagging
- Tantrums
- Nervous cough
- Nervous laughter

APPENDIX 3: OFFENCES AGAINST CHILDREN

- The murder of a child or young person under 18
- Common assault and battery
- Infanticide
- Child destruction
- Manslaughter of a child or young person under 18
- The abandonment or exposure of a child under 2 so as to endanger its life or health
- Cruelty to a person under 16, including assault, ill-treatment or neglect
- Allowing a person under 16 to be in a brothel
- Causing or allowing a person under 16 to be used for begging
- Exposing a child under 7 to risk of burning
- Allowing a person under 16 to take part in a dangerous performance
- Rape or attempted rape of a girl under 18
- Procurement or attempted procurement of a girl under 18 by threats
- Procurement of a girl under 18 by false pretences
- Administering drugs to a girl under 18 to obtain or facilitate intercourse
- Intercourse or attempted intercourse with a girl under 13
- Intercourse or attempted intercourse with a girl between 13 and 16
- Incest or attempt to commit incest by a man against a female, where the victim is under 18
- Incest or attempt to commit incest by a woman, where the victim is under 18
- Buggery or attempt to commit buggery with a person under 18
- Indecency between men where one or both is under 18
- Indecent assault on a girl under 18
- Indecent assault on a male under 18
- Assault with intent to commit buggery
- Abduction of an unmarried girl under 16 from a parent or guardian
- Causing or attempting to cause prostitution of a girl under 18
- Procuration or attempted procuration of a girl under 18
- Detention of a girl in a brothel or other premises
- Permitting a girl under 16 to use premises for intercourse
- Causing or encouraging prostitution of, intercourse with, or indecent assault on a girl under 16
- Indecent conduct towards a child under 14
- Aiding, abetting, counselling or procuring the suicide of a person under 18

APPENDIX 4: FLOW CHARTS: WHAT TO DO

Flow chart 1: Referral

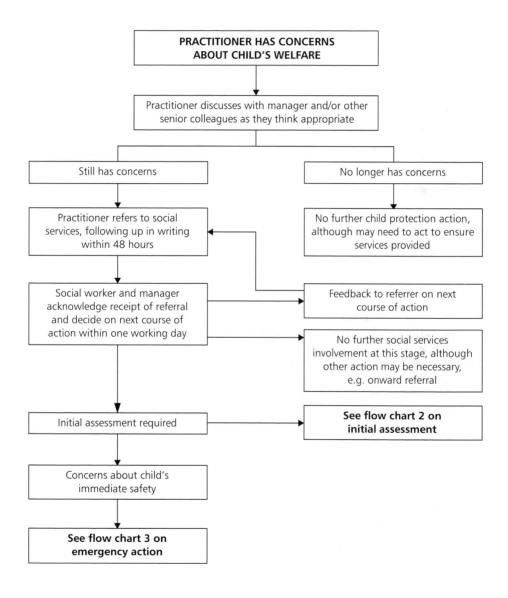

Flow chart 2: What happens following initial assessment

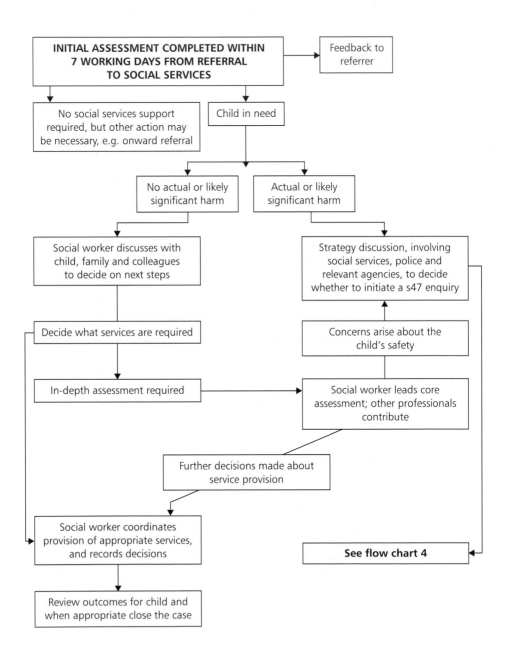

INITIAL ASSESSMENT COMPLETED WITHIN 7 WORKING DAYS FROM REFERRAL TO SOCIAL SERVICES

Feedback to referrer

No social services support required, but other action may be necessary, e.g. onward referral

Child in need

No actual or likely significant harm

Actual or likely significant harm

Social worker discusses with child, family and colleagues to decide on next steps

Strategy discussion, involving social services, police and relevant agencies, to decide whether to initiate a s47 enquiry

Decide what services are required

Concerns arise about the child's safety

In-depth assessment required

Social worker leads core assessment; other professionals contribute

Further decisions made about service provision

Social worker coordinates provision of appropriate services, and records decisions

See flow chart 4

Review outcomes for child and when appropriate close the case

Flow chart 3: Urgent action to safeguard children

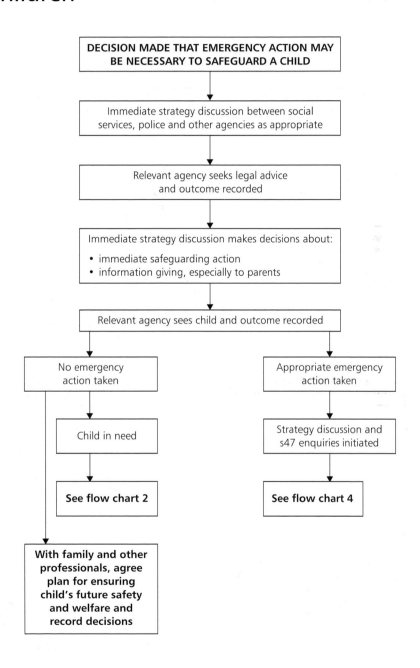

DECISION MADE THAT EMERGENCY ACTION MAY BE NECESSARY TO SAFEGUARD A CHILD

Immediate strategy discussion between social services, police and other agencies as appropriate

Relevant agency seeks legal advice and outcome recorded

Immediate strategy discussion makes decisions about:
- immediate safeguarding action
- information giving, especially to parents

Relevant agency sees child and outcome recorded

No emergency action taken

Child in need

See flow chart 2

With family and other professionals, agree plan for ensuring child's future safety and welfare and record decisions

Appropriate emergency action taken

Strategy discussion and s47 enquiries initiated

See flow chart 4

Flow chart 4: What happens after the strategy discussion

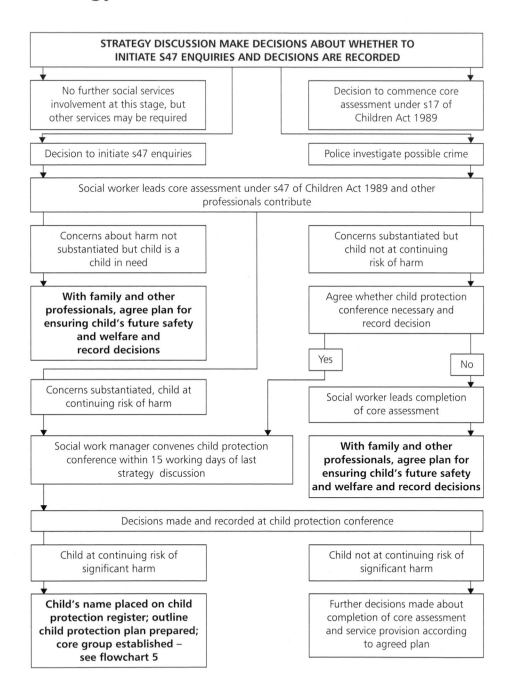

STRATEGY DISCUSSION MAKE DECISIONS ABOUT WHETHER TO INITIATE S47 ENQUIRIES AND DECISIONS ARE RECORDED

No further social services involvement at this stage, but other services may be required

Decision to commence core assessment under s17 of Children Act 1989

Decision to initiate s47 enquiries

Police investigate possible crime

Social worker leads core assessment under s47 of Children Act 1989 and other professionals contribute

Concerns about harm not substantiated but child is a child in need

Concerns substantiated but child not at continuing risk of harm

With family and other professionals, agree plan for ensuring child's future safety and welfare and record decisions

Agree whether child protection conference necessary and record decision

Yes

No

Concerns substantiated, child at continuing risk of harm

Social worker leads completion of core assessment

Social work manager convenes child protection conference within 15 working days of last strategy discussion

With family and other professionals, agree plan for ensuring child's future safety and welfare and record decisions

Decisions made and recorded at child protection conference

Child at continuing risk of significant harm

Child not at continuing risk of significant harm

Child's name placed on child protection register; outline child protection plan prepared; core group established – see flowchart 5

Further decisions made about completion of core assessment and service provision according to agreed plan

Flow chart 5: What happens after the child protection conference

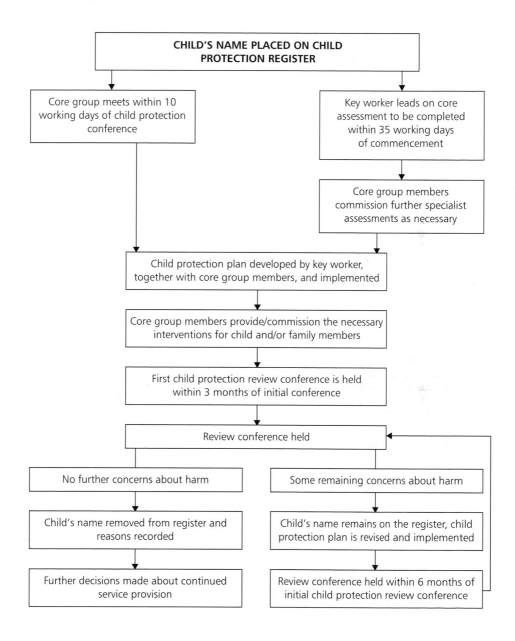

CHILD'S NAME PLACED ON CHILD PROTECTION REGISTER

Core group meets within 10 working days of child protection conference

Key worker leads on core assessment to be completed within 35 working days of commencement

Core group members commission further specialist assessments as necessary

Child protection plan developed by key worker, together with core group members, and implemented

Core group members provide/commission the necessary interventions for child and/or family members

First child protection review conference is held within 3 months of initial conference

Review conference held

No further concerns about harm

Some remaining concerns about harm

Child's name removed from register and reasons recorded

Child's name remains on the register, child protection plan is revised and implemented

Further decisions made about continued service provision

Review conference held within 6 months of initial child protection review conference

APPENDIX 5: CHILD PROTECTION POLICY

Bovingdon Primary School

Child Protection Policy

1. INTRODUCTION

Bovingdon Primary school fully recognises its responsibilities for child protection.
Our Policy applies to all staff, governors and volunteers working in the school.
There are five main elements to our policy.

> Ensuring we practice safe recruitment in checking the suitability of staff and volunteers to work with children.
>
> Raising awareness of child protection issues and equipping children with the skills needed to keep them safe.
>
> Developing and then implementing procedures for identifying and reporting cases, or suspected cases, of abuse.
>
> Supporting pupils who have been abused in accordance with his/her agreed child protection plan.
>
> Establishing a safe environment in which children can learn and develop.

We recognise that because of the day to day contact with children, school staff are well placed to observe the outward signs of abuse. The school will therefore:

> Establish and maintain an environment where children feel secure, are encouraged to talk, and are listened to.
>
> Ensure children know that there are adults in the school whom they can approach if they are worried.
>
> Include opportunities in the PSHE curriculum for children to develop the skills they need to recognise and stay safe from abuse.

We will follow the procedures set out by the Area Child Protection Committee and take account of guidance issued by the Department for Education and Skills to:

> Ensure we have a designated teacher for child protection who has received appropriate training and support for this role.
>
> Ensure we have a nominated governor responsible for child protection.
>
> Ensure every member of staff, volunteer and governor knows the name of the designated teacher responsible for child protection and their role.
>
> Ensure all staff and volunteers understand their responsibilities in being alert to the signs of abuse and responsibility for referring any concerns to the designated teacher responsible for child protection.
>
> Ensure that parents have an understanding of the responsibility placed on the school and staff for child protection by setting out its obligations in the school prospectus.

Notify social services if there is an unexplained absence of more than two days of a pupil who is on the child protection register.

Develop effective links with relevant agencies and co-operate as required with their enquiries regarding child protection matters including attendance at case conferences.

Keep written records of concerns about children, even where there is no need to refer the matter immediately.

Ensure all records are kept securely, separate from the main pupil file, and in locked locations.

Develop and then follow procedures where an allegation is made against a member of staff or volunteer.

Ensure safe recruitment practices are always followed.

We recognise that children who are abused or witness violence may find it difficult to develop a sense of self worth. They may feel helplessness, humiliation and some sense of blame. The school may be the only stable, secure and predictable element in the lives of children at risk. When at school their behaviour may be challenging and defiant or they may be withdrawn. The school will endeavour to support the pupil through:

The content of the curriculum.

The school ethos which promotes a positive, supportive and secure environment and gives pupils a sense of being valued.

The school behaviour policy which is aimed at supporting vulnerable pupils in the school. The school will ensure that the pupil knows that some behaviour is unacceptable but they are valued and not to be blamed for any abuse which has occurred.

Liaison with other agencies that support the pupil such as social services, Child and Adult Mental Health Service, education welfare service and educational psychology service.

Ensuring that, where a pupil on the child protection register leaves, their information is transferred to the new school immediately and that the child's social worker is informed.

Hertfordshire Child Protection Procedures

The school follows the procedures contained in the Hertfordshire Child Protection Committee's "Child Protection" – a guide to procedure and practice for all professional staff in Hertfordshire who work with children.

School Staff

Teachers and other school staff are particularly well placed to observe outward signs of abuse, changes in behaviour and failure to develop because they have daily contact with the children. Staff should be aware of the important role the school has in the early recognition of the signs and symptoms of abuse or neglect and be familiar with the appropriate referral process.

Ethos of the School

The school aims to develop an ethos in which children feel secure, their viewpoints are valued, they are encouraged to talk and are listened to.

2. MISSION STATEMENT

Bovingdon Primary School is concerned about the welfare and safety of all its pupils and attempts to create an ethos in which pupils feel secure, valued, listened to and are taken seriously.

4. THE DESIGNATED TEACHER/GOVERNOR

The Designated Teachers for Child Protection are _____ and _____.
Their role is to:

- Ensure that the Hertfordshire Child Protection Committee's procedures are followed throughout the school
- Ensure that all staff are aware of these procedures
- Ensure that appropriate training and support is provided to all staff
- Ensure that the Headteacher is kept fully informed of any concerns
- Develop effective working relationships with other agencies and services
- Decide whether to take further action about specific concerns (e.g. refer to Social Services)
- Liaise with Social Services teams over suspected cases of child abuse
- Ensure that accurate records relating to individual children are kept in a secure place and marked "Strictly Confidential"
- Submit reports to, and attend Child Protection Conferences
- Ensure that the school effectively monitors children who have been identified as "at risk"
- Provide guidance to parents, children and staff about obtaining suitable support

The designated School Governor for child protection is _____. The Governing body are responsible for ensuring that the school has effective policies and procedures in place and for monitoring the school's implementation of its policies and its compliance with current legislation.

5. SCHOOL PROCEDURES

If any member of staff is concerned about a child he or she must inform the designated teacher(s) for child protection (currently _____ and _____).

Information regarding the concerns must be recorded by the member of staff on the same day. The recording must be a clear, precise, factual account of the observations.

The designated teacher, _____ or _____, will decide whether the concerns should be referred to the Social Services department. If it is decided to make a referral to Social Serices this will be done without prior discussion with the parents.

If a referral is made to Social Services, the designated teacher will ensure that a written report of the conerns is sent to the social worker dealing with the case within 48 hours.

Particular attention will be paid to the attendance and development of any child who has been identified as "at risk" or who has been placed on the Child Protection Register.

If a pupil who is known to be on the Child Protection Register changes school, the designated teacher(s) for child protection, _____ or _____, will inform the social worker responsible for the case and transfer the appropriate records to the receiving school.

6. WHEN TO BE CONCERNED

Staff should be concerned about a pupil if he or she:

- Has any injury which is not typical of the bumps and scrapes normally associated with children's injuries
- Regularly has unexplained injuries
- Frequently has injuries (even when apparently reasonable explanations are given)
- Gives confusing or conflicting explanations on how injuries were sustained
- Exhibits significant changes in beahviour, performance or attitude
- Indulges in sexual behaviour which is unusually explicit and/or inappropriate to his or her age
- Discloses an experience in which he or she may have been significantly harmed

7. DEALING WITH A DISCLOSURE

If a pupil discloses that he or she has been abused in some way, the member of staff should:

- Listen to what is being said without displaying shock or disbelief
- Accept what is being said
- Allow the child to talk freely
- Reassure the child but not make promises which it might not be possible to keep
- Not promise confidentiality – it might be necessary to refer to Social Services
- Reassure him or her that what has happened is not his or her fault
- Impress upon them that it was the right thing to tell
- Listen, rather than ask direct questions
- Ask open questions rather than leading questions
- Not criticise the alleged perpetrator
- Explain what has to be done next and who has to be told

8. RECORD KEEPING

When a pupil has made a disclosure the member of staff should:

- Make brief notes as soon as possible after the conversation
- Not destroy the original notes in case they are needed by a court
- Pass a copy of your notes to the Headteacher
- Record the date, time, place and any noticeable non-verbal behaviour and the words used by the child
- Draw a diagram to indicate the position of any bruising or other injury

- Record statements and observations rather than interpretations or assumptions

9. SUPPORT
Dealing with a disclosure from a child, and a Child Protection case in general, is likely to be a stressful experience. The member of staff should, therefore, consider seeking support for him/herself and discuss this with _____ or _____.

10. ALLEGATIONS INVOLVING SCHOOL STAFF
If a child, or parent, makes a complaint of abuse against a member of staff, the person receiving the complaint must take it seriously and immediately inform the Headteacher.

Any member of staff who has reason to suspect that a pupil may have been abused by another member of staff, either at school or elsewhere, must immediately inform the Headteacher. He or she shuld also make a record of the concerns including a note of anyone else who witnessed the incident or allegation.

If the concerns are about the Headteacher, the Head of Education Welfare Service must be contacted.

The Headteacher will not investigate the allegation itself, or take written or detailed statements, but he/she must make a referral direct to the local Social Services team. If the allegation constitutes a serious criminal offence it will be necessary to contact Social Services before informing the member of staff.

If it is decided that it is not necessary to refer to Social Services the Headteacher will consider whether there needs to be an intenal investigation.

11. CONFIDENTIALITY
DFEE Circular 10/95 acknowledges that child protection raises issues of confidentiality and must be clearly understoof by all staff in the Education service. The circular advises that all staff in the Education department, both teaching and non-teaching, have a "responsibility to share relevant information about the protection of children with other professionals, particularly the investigative agencies (Social Services and Police). If a child confides in a member of staff and requests that the information is kept secret, it is important that the member of staff tells the child that he or she has a responsibility to refer cases of alleged abuse to the appropraite agencies for the chid's sake. Within that context, the child should be assured that the matter will be disclosed only to people who need to know about it. Staff who receive information about children and their families in the course of their work should share that information only within appropriate professional contexts Child Protection records should be kept securely locked."

12. PARENTAL GUIDANCE
Parents who are concerned about any aspect of this policy or about any issues of child protection in general, should discuss their concerns directly with the Headteacher.

Parents who wish to make a complaint about the manner in which the school has implemented the above procedures can do so by following the guidelines as set out in the School's Complaints Procedure (a copy can be obtained via the school office).

References   Hertfordshire Area Child Protection Committee Child Protection Multi Agency Procedures:
Section 8b – Allegations of Abuse Involving Staff in Schools
Appendix 13 – Guidance for Headteacher about what actions/behaviour should be referred through Child Protection Procedures.

DFEE Document 10/95. Section 44–52

APPENDIX 6: RESOURCES

Further reading

Barker, J and Hodes, D. (2007) *The Child in Mind: A Child Protection Handbook*, 3rd edn. Routledge, London.

Fawcett, B. *et al.* (2004) *Contemporary Childcare Policy and Practice*. Palgrave, Basingstoke.

Lawrence, A. (2004) *Principles of Child Protection*. Oxford University Press, Oxford.

Munro, E. (2008) *Effective Child Protection*, 2nd edn. Sage, London.

Walker, A. (2008) *Possessing the Secret of Joy*. New Press, London.

Organisations: helplines and websites

ChildLine
Telephone: 0800 1111
Web: www.childline.org.uk

Child Poverty Action Group
94 White Lion Street
London N1
Telephone: 020 7837 7979
Web: www.cpag.org.uk

Children Are Unbeatable!
Telephone: 020 7713 0569
Web: www.childrenareunbeatable.org.uk

Children's Legal Centre
University of Essex
Wivenhoe Park
Colchester
Essex CO4 3SQ
Telephone: 01206 873 820
Web: www.childrenslegalcentre.com

The Children's Society
Edward Rudolph House
Margery Street
London WC1X 0JL
Telephone: 0845 300 1128
Web: www.childrens-society.org.uk

Contact a Family (for families with disabled children)
209 City Road
London EC1 1JN
Telephone: 020 7608 8700
Web: www.cafamily.org.uk

Criminal Records Bureau
PO Box 110
Liverpool L69 3EF
Telephone: 0870 9090 811
Web: www.crb.gov.uk

Cry-Sis (counselling advice if your baby cries excessively)
27 Old Gloucester Street
London WC1N 3XX
Telephone: 08451 228 669
Web: www.cry-sis.org.uk

Refuge
Telephone: 0808 2000 247
Web: www.refuge.org.uk

Exploring Parenthood (aims to reduce family stress)
4 Ivory Place
20a Threadgold Street
London W11 4BP
Telephone: 020 7221 4471

Gingerbread (help for single parents)
255 Kentish Road
London NW5 2LX
Telephone: 020 7428 5400
Web: www.gingerbread.org.uk

Home-Start UK (practical help for distressed families)
2 Salisbury Road
Leicester LE1 7QR
Telephone: 0116 233 9955 (or see local directory)
Web: www.home-start.org.uk

Kidscape
2 Grosvenor Gardens
London SW15 0DH
Telephone: 020 7730 3300
Web: www.kidscape.org.uk

Meet-a-Mum Association (for mothers suffering from post-natal depression)
Telephone: 0845 120 3746
www.mama.co.uk

National Children's Bureau
8 Wakely Street
London EC1V 7QE
Telephone: 020 7843 6000
Web: www.ncb.org

Family Welfare Association
501–505 Kingsland Road
London E8 4AU
Telephone: 020 7254 6251
Web: www.family-action.org.uk

NSPCC
42 Curtain Road
London EC2A 3NH
Telephone: 0800 800 500
Web: www.nspcc.org.uk

Parentline Plus
Unit 520
Highgate Studios
53–79 Highgate Road
London NW5 1TL
Telephone: 020 7284 5500
Web: www.parentlineplus.org.uk

Relate
Telephone: 0300 100 1234
Web: www.relate.org.uk

Save the Children Fund
1 St John's Lane
London EC1M 4AR
Telephone: 020 7012 6400

Training resources

NSPCC (2003) *Learning to Protect*. A training pack to support schools. For more information contact: learningresources@nspcc.org.uk
NSPCC. *Educare*. Distance learning materials about child protection. www.nspcc.org.uk

INDEX

Page numbers in *italics* indicate figures or tables